REDEEMED BY GOD - 3
God's Redemption through Jesus, and His Plan for Eternity
3rd Edition

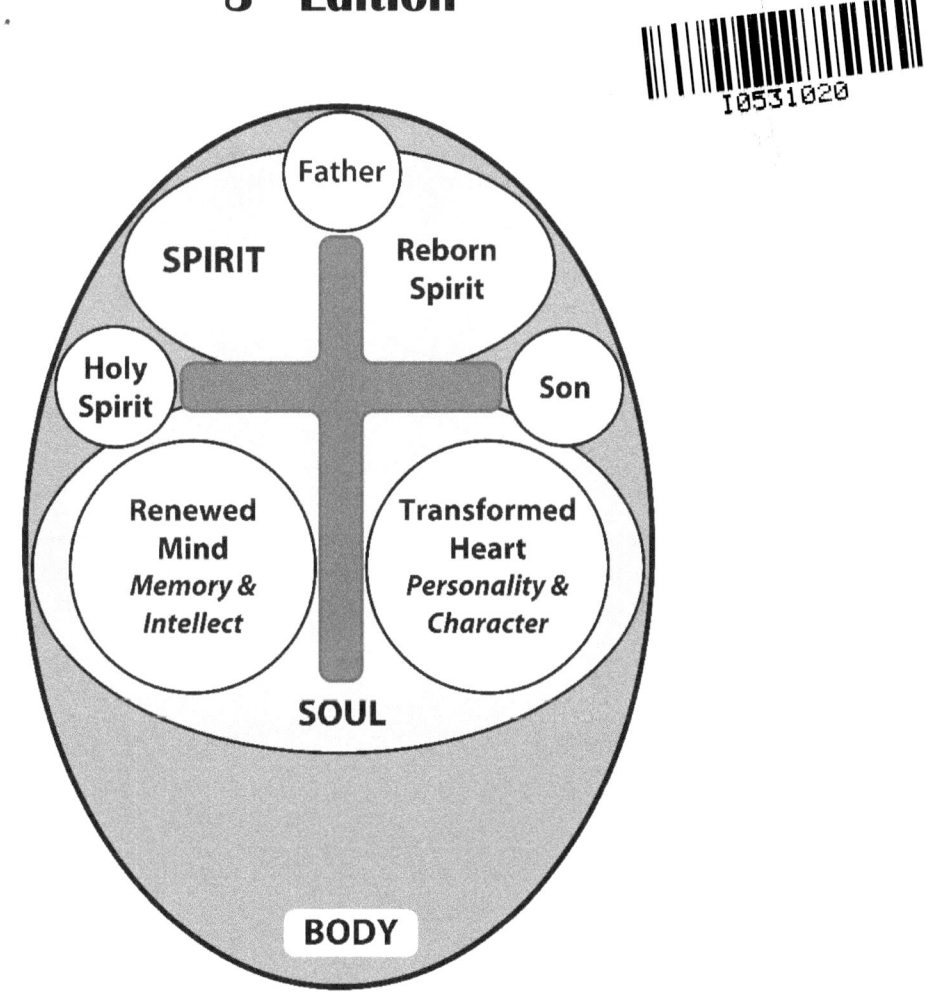

By
Douglas D. Reynolds, Ph.D.

ISBN: 978-1-960093-64-6 (Paperback)
ISBN: 978-1-960093-65-3 (eBook)

Scriptures taken from the NEW AMERICAN STANDARD BIBLE® Copyright © 1960, 1962, 1963, 1968, 1971, 1972, 1973, 1975, 1977, 1995, 2020 by the Lockman Foundation. Used with permission.

Book Ordering Information:
Atticus Publishing
548 Market St PMB 70756
San Francisco, CA 94104
(888) 208-9296
info@atticuspublishing.com
www.atticuspublishing.com

Printed in the United States of America

TITLE PAGE IMAGE

The apostle Paul stated in 1 Thessalonians 5:23 we are born with a spirit, soul and body. The outer ellipse in the title page image represents our physical body. Our body interacts with the physical world through our five physical senses of sight, hearing, touch, taste, and smell. The two inner ellipses in the outer ellipse of the body represent our spirit and soul. Our spirit gives life to our physical body and interacts with the spiritual realm where God exists. Our soul functions through our body and spirit as we interact with the physical world and the spiritual realm. Our spirit and soul are integrally linked. Our body dies and returns to dust when our spirit no longer can support physical life. Our spirit and soul continue in an eternal existence beyond physical death. They continue either in the kingdom of heaven in the presence of God, Jesus and the Holy Spirit or separated from Them in Hades (hell) before and in the lake of fire after the great white throne judgement.

Our soul is comprised of our mind and heart. Our mind is the seat of our memory and intellect. Our memory is the repository of information and experiences we have processed and assimilated throughout our life. Our intellect is the knowledge and wisdom we acquire from this information and these experiences. Our heart is the seat of our personality and character. Our personality is the organized pattern of behavioral characteristics that identify and define who we are. Our character defines the moral and ethical qualities of our personality.

Our soul possesses memory, acquires knowledge, experiences emotions, creates thoughts, forms habits, and initiates actions through our body and spirit. It develops as our mind and heart process and assimilate information it receives through our life experiences. It controls how we encounter, interpret and respond to new life experiences based on how it has processed and assimilated information it has received from prior life experiences.

The Bible teaches we relate to God as Father, Son and Holy Spirit. There are three eternal Persons within the Godhead even though there is one God. They each possess all the eternal attributes of God and interact with perfect agreement. However, they relate to and interact with us in distinct and unique ways. God, the Father, is our Creator and the One who is behind everything and to whom everyone in heaven and on earth is accountable. God's Son, Jesus, is our Lord and Savior. He is the One for and through whom all things have been created and are held together and through whom we approach God, the Father. The Holy Spirit, our Comforter and Helper, reveals the mind of God to us and makes our needs and requests known to God, the Father, through our prayers.

The Bible teaches we are born into this world with a sin nature that separates us from God. We are born spiritually dead because God's spirit is not present in us. However, the

Bible also teaches God loves us, desires to commune and fellowship with us, and is active in us through the Holy Spirit. The Holy Spirit makes us aware of sins in our life, leads us to repent of these sins, and creates a desire within us to enter a relationship with God. God has made this relationship possible through the sacrificial death and resurrection of Jesus. God extends His mercy and grace to us, and He makes known to us His desire to redeem and reconcile us to Himself through Jesus' death and resurrection. However, we must seek God's grace and forgiveness and acknowledge and repent of our sins to enter a reconciled relationship with Him through Jesus. God loves and forgives us, and He communes and fellowships with us when we approach Him through Jesus.

Jesus stated in John 14:6 we can only approach God, the Father, through Him. Therefore, being a good, moral and generous person independent of a relationship with God through Jesus does not gain us entrance into the kingdom of God while we are alive, nor does this gain us entrance into the kingdom of heaven after we die. God redeems and reconciles us to Himself through our faith and trust in and obedience to Jesus as a gift. This gift for us is free because we can do nothing to earn or obtain it independent of our relationship with God through Jesus. The Holy Spirit leads us to repent of our sins, profess with our mouth Jesus is Lord, and believe in our heart God raised Him from the dead to receive God's salvation through His gift of grace (Romans 10:9-10). This saves us from eternal separation from God, Jesus and the Holy Spirit after we die. We are spiritually reborn because God's Spirit along with Jesus and the Holy Spirit take up residence in us.

Paul instructed us in 1 Corinthians 3:10 - 15 to build our life on the foundation of Jesus. We begin building this foundation by reading and study God's word in the Bible. The Holy Spirit opens our mind to understand and internalize what we read and study in the Bible. Our mind is renewed as we internalize and assimilate the words Jesus spoke in the four Gospels, and the Holy Spirit enters our heart to transform our personality and character as our mind is renewed. We are transformed into the person God has created us to be as we continue to have faith in and trust Jesus and become obedient to the words He spoke in the four Gospels.

To the members of my family
my wife, Linda;
my son and daughter-in-law, John and Latricia, and son, Jeff (deceased);
my granddaughters, Janet, Jennifer and Ashlin;
my grandson, Jerry; and
my great grandchildren, Jered, Michael, Hailey,
Alex, Dustin, Ian, Mason and Jackson.

To the Rev. James "JD" Hilliard who reviewed the manuscript for this book and provided helpful recommendations for its improvement.

TABLE OF CONTENTS

PREFACE

ACTIONS OF THE HOLY SPIRIT IN MY LIFE

God through the Holy Spirit indicated in 1982 He wanted me to write a book that addressed spiritual life principles associated with His word in the Bible. My initial response was why me? I am a Ph.D. mechanical engineer. I am not a pastor, Bible scholar or theologian. The Holy Spirit initiated a process when I committed to write this book that would enable and equip me to write and publish it. 2 Timothy 3:16-17 motivated me as I engaged in this process. Paul stated:

> "All Scripture is inspired by God and profitable for teaching, for reproof, for correction, for training in righteousness, so that the man of God may be adequate, equipped for every good work."

I again received God's call in 2000 for me to be one of His servants. He indicated He would reveal to me by my reading and studying the Bible and through the Holy Spirit an understanding of Scriptures related to the future. 2 Peter 1:20-21 provided significance to this understanding. Peter stated:

> "But know this first of all, that no prophecy of Scripture is a matter of one's own interpretation, for no prophecy was ever made by an act of human will, but men moved by the Holy Spirit spoke from God."

God indicated difficult days will arise in the future, and He wanted me to be a messenger who shares this understanding with others. He indicated He will be with and support those who trust and have faith in Jesus and obey His words. I believe the future God referred to in 2000 is now here.

The Holy Spirit has revealed to me through the Bible and life experiences the love God extends to us through Jesus and Him. He has helped me to understand the:

- Significance of the infinite sacrifice God made for us through the sacrificial death and resurrection of His Son, Jesus:
- Significance of the infinite sacrifice Jesus made through His death and shed blood on a cross so God, His Father, can redeem us;

- Importance of our receiving the redemption and reconciliation God extends to us through His grace and our faith and trust in and obedience to Jesus; and
- Significance of God's holiness in the context of His relationship with His creation and with us through Jesus.

God will execute His justice that is an extension of His holiness when we stand before and are judged by Jesus on the last day.

I initially wrote and published three books in response to the leadership of the Holy Spirit. My first book, *REDEEMED BY GOD, Our Relationship with God through His Son, Jesus Christ*, was published in 2003. This book addressed the:

- The nature and character of God as Father, Son and Holy Spirit;
- The nature and character of Satan and sin;
- The nature of our creation as spirit, soul and body;
- Spiritual death we experience because of sin;
- Spiritual rebirth and life we receive from God by means of His grace extended to us through our faith and trust in and obedience to Jesus;
- Spiritual growth we experience through Bible study, prayer and a transformed heart;
- Spiritual gifts the Holy Spirit gives to us to enable and equip us to engage in ministry and service to others;
- Spiritual life principles that equip us to effectively address life challenges;
- The Christian Church through which we engage in ministry and service to others; and
- The seven-year tribulation through which God will execute His judgement on a fallen and rebellious world that has rejected Him, Jesus and the Holy Spirit.

The Holy Spirit led me in 2013 to revise and separate my original book into two books:

- *REDEEMED BY GOD - 1, Spiritual Growth and Life Principles Associated with the Gospel of Jesus*, and
- REDEEMED BY GOD - 2, A Christian Perspective of the End Time and a New World Order.

These books were published in 2015. Discussion on the seven-year tribulation was placed in *REDEEMED BY GOD – 2, A Christian Perspective of the End Time and a New World Order* with discussions on the:

- Nature and character of God and Satan,

- Functions of our soul and spirit,

- Our relationship with God through our faith and trust in and obedience to Jesus, and

- Events associated with the establishment of a New World Order.

This book introduced cultural conflicts between secular humanism and Christianity, progressivism and conservatism, and socialism and capitalism. These conflicts and their consequences are evident today in the United States and other countries. They will lead to the formation of a New World Order. The topics covered in *REDEEMED BY GOD, Our Relationship with God through His Son, Jesus Christ* without material on the seven-year tribulation were revised and presented in *REDEEMED BY GOD – 1, Spiritual Growth and Life Principles Associated with the Gospel of Jesus*. Two subsequent revised editions of these two books were published.

    REDEEMED BY GOD – 1 and *REDEEMED BY GOD -2* were updated and re-released in 2020 as part of the three-book series with titles:

- *REDEEMED BY GOD – 1, Spiritual Life Principles Associated with God's Word*;

- *REDEEMED BY GOD – 2, Time of the End, Return of Jesus and a New World Order*; and

- *REDEEMED BY GOD – 3, God's Redemption through Jesus and His Plan for Eternity.*

The new releases of *REDEEMED BY GOD – 1* and *REDEEMED BY GOD – 2* contained revised materials presented in their prior releases. *REDEEMED BY GOD – 3* was condensed from *REDEEMED BY GOD – 2* and addressed the:

- Nature and character of God and Satan;

- Origin and nature of sin;

- Nature of our creation as spirit, soul and body;

- Functions of our soul and spirit;

- Our relationship with God through our faith and trust in and obedience to Jesus;

- God's future judgments of the unrighteous and righteous; and

- The destruction of the existing heaven and earth and the creation of a new heaven, earth and Jerusalem.

Revised 2nd editions of the above three *REDEEMED BY GOD* books were published in 2024.

My *REDEEMED BY GOD* books were written from an evangelical perspective of what I perceived the Bible was saying to and teaching me. My writing style as a Ph.D. mechanical engineer is that of a technical writer. Cultural influences on non-biblical topics in *REDEEMED BY GOD – 2* were addressed. This was not done in *REDEEMED BY GOD – 1* and *REDEEMED BY GOD - 3*.

My *REDEEMED BY GOD* books have been written for individuals who are struggling to cope with real life situations related to the cultural conflicts that are occurring in the world. Many are seeking a relationship with God through Jesus and the Holy Spirit to better equip themselves to address these conflicts and the life struggles they are creating. The revised 2nd edition releases of my *REDEEMED BY GOD* books are written for individuals who:

- Have entered a reconciled relationship with God through their faith and trust in and obedience to Jesus and want to grow and mature in this relationship through the presence of the Holy Spirit in their lives (*REDEEMED BY GOD – 1*);
- Have entered a reconciled relationship with God through their faith and trust in and obedience to Jesus and want to grow in their knowledge and understanding of events that will lead to the formation of a New World Order and the seven-year tribulation (*REDEEMED BY GOD – 2*); and
- Do not know God but who the Holy Spirit is nudging to seek and enter a redeemed relationship with Him through Jesus (*REDEEMED BY GOD -3*).

Bible scriptures are presented in these books to document that the spiritual life principle and precepts addressed in my books are from God. These Bible scriptures have been selected to aid in the spiritual growth of those who read my books.

SPIRITUAL ORIGIN OF TODAY'S CULTURAL CONFLICTS

The cultural conflicts addressed in *REDEEMED BY GOD - 2* are being discussed and framed today as a conflict between the progressive left and the conservative right. What is not being discussed is the spiritual origin of these conflicts. This origin is traced back to ancient secret societies that existed at the time of the Tower of Babel and after its fall described in Genesis 11:1-9. These secret societies opposed God and were led by illuminists who were the intellectual elite of their day. These illuminists were disciples of Lucifer and had as their objectives the:

- Absolute rule over the world,
- Elimination of private prosperity,
- Elimination of religions, and

- Elimination of nation-states.

These objectives after the death and resurrection of Jesus found their way into later anti-Christian secret societies that included the Luciferians, Rosicrucians and the Levellers. They eventually found their way into a secret society called the Illuminati.

The Illuminati controlled global movement was made popular by Adam Weishaupt during the latter part of the 18th century. The Illuminati wanted to establish a deistic, global and dictatorial government that will abolish:

- Governments of all nation-states;
- All private property;
- All inheritance rights;
- Patriotism to national causes;
- Social relationships within families,
- Sexual prohibition laws and moral codes; and
- Religious disciplines based on faith in a transcendent God, while promoting faith in nature, man and reason.

These objectives have been incorporated into the progressive left agenda that opposes the presence of God, Jesus and the Holy Spirit in our lives and culture.

SIGNIFICANCE OF GOD'S GRACE

I mention in my REDEEMED BY GOD books that we enter a redeemed relationship with God through our **faith** and **trust** in and **obedience** to Jesus. **Faith** is our strong belief in the **truth** of the Bible's discussions regarding our relationship with God and the roles Jesus and the Holy Spirit play in this relationship. **Trust** is our assured reliance on this **truth** and on God's and Jesus' ability to honor Their covenants and promises presented in the Bible. **Obedience** is our submission to the reality and requirements of this **truth** on our life and to God's laws and the words Jesus spoke in the four Gospels.

Paul stated in Ephesians 2:8 we are saved by God's **grace** through **faith**. God's **grace** is His conscious and deliberate extension of His love and good will to provide us with something we can neither earn nor provide for ourself. Paul stated God extends His **grace** to us as a gift, and he referred to this gift as being free in Romans 5:15-17. God extends His **grace** to and redeems us with no cost to us because we can do nothing to obtain it independent of His love for us, and so we cannot claim we are entitled to His grace because of actions we initiate.

Paul continued in Ephesians 2:9 we cannot be redeemed by our own works independent of God's **grace**. He then stated in Ephesians 2:10 we become new creations by God in Christ Jesus to perform **good works** He has prepared beforehand for us to perform.

We are redeemed by God's **grace** when we profess with our mouth Jesus is Lord and believe in our heart God raised Him from the dead (Romans 10:8-10). The Holy Spirit then begins to reside in us, and we enter a bilateral relationship with God through Jesus and the presence of the Holy Spirit in our life. God, Jesus, the Holy Spirit and we have obligations in a relationship that results from our being redeemed by God's **grace**. We can **trust** God and Jesus to honor their covenants and promises regarding our relationship with Them that are presented in the Bible. We are to develop, grow and mature in our **faith** and **trust** in and **obedience** to Jesus with the assistance of the Holy Spirit in our relationship with God through Jesus.

Paul indicated in Romans 10:17 **faith** comes from hearing and proceeds from the words of Jesus. The Holy Spirit in our life facilitates the development and growth of our **faith** as we hear and are taught the words of Jesus in the four Gospels. These words, as we internalize them, facilitate the development and growth of our **faith** through a process that transforms our life by renewing our mind (Romans 12:2). Renewing our mind transforms our life choice from being defined and determined by our culture to being defined and determined by the words of Jesus.

Our **faith and trust in and obedience to Jesus develop, grow and mature as we:**

- Read, study and internalize God's word in the Bible (1 Peter 2:1–3);
- Incorporate the spiritual life principles associated with God's word in the Bible into our life (1 Timothy 4:13–16);
- Grow and mature in our relationship with God through Jesus and the presence of the Holy Spirit in our life (Philippians 2:12–13);
- **Obey** the words Jesus spoke in the four Gospels (John 14:15, 21, 23); and
- Do **good works** God has prepared for us to perform (Ephesians 2:10). The Holy Spirit, as we study and internalize the words of Jesus, equips us with unique supernatural spiritual gifts that enable us to perform **good works** God prepares for us to perform (Romans 12:4-8, 1 Corinthians 12:3-11, 28, and Ephesians 4:11-13).

We do **good works** because Jesus instructed us in Matthew 5:16:

> "Let your light shine before men in such a way that they may see your **good works**, and glorify your Father who is in heaven."

We do **good works** because Paul stated in Ephesians 2:10:

> "For we are [God's] workmanship, created in Christ Jesus for **good works**, which [He] prepared beforehand so that we would walk in them."

He affirmed in 2 Timothy 3:16–17 our understanding of the Bible enables and equips us to do the **good works** Jesus instructed and God has prepared for us to perform.

God through Jesus and the Holy Spirit draws us close to Himself to receive and grow in His love. The Holy Spirit motivates us to engage in the above activities to spiritually grow and mature in our relationship with God through Jesus. He enables us to love, minister to and serve others in Jesus' name. This equips us to perform **good works** out of love for God and others in **obedience** to Jesus with guidance from the Holy Spirit. God and Jesus bless and reward us when we engage in activities to spiritually grow and mature, and we perform **good works** Jesus instructs and God prepares for us to perform. However, we risk losing Their blessings and rewards when we fail to engage in activities to spiritually grow and mature, and we do none of the **good works** Jesus instructs and God prepares for us to perform after we have entered our relationship with Them (John 15:1–11).

GOOD WORKS

Our good works are fruit that proceeds from the vine of Jesus (John 15:1–6). They are activities God prepares for us to perform (Ephesian 2:10) to glorify Himself (Matthew 5:16). Good works are our response of love and obedience for receiving the gift of grace and redemption God extends to us through Jesus, and they are an integral part of our relationship with God through Jesus. They:

- Are our love-offerings to God that we extend to others (2 Timothy 2:15);
- Are performed to glorify God (Matthew 5:16);
- Are positions of leadership and service we perform in and through our local church (Ephesians 4:11-13);
- Are how we minister to and serve the needs of others (1 Peter 4:10).
- Are our witness to those who have not received Jesus as their Lord and Savior (Hebrews 13:2);
- Are our witness to fellow Christians (Colossians 3:16).
- Show we are God's workmanship, created in Christ Jesus to perform good works (Ephesians 2:10); and
- Reveal the presence of the Holy Spirit in our life (Matthew 5:14-16).

The Holy Spirits provides us with supernatural spiritual gifts that enable and equip us to perform our good works (Romans 12:4-8, 1 Corinthians 12:3-11, 28, and Ephesians 4:11-13). Paul instructed us in 1 Timothy 4:14-16:

> "Do not neglect the spiritual gift within you, which was bestowed on you through prophetic utterance with the laying on of hands by the presbytery. Take pains with these things; be absorbed in them that your progress will be evident to all. Pay close attention to yourself and to your teaching; persevere in these things, for as you do this you will ensure salvation both for yourself and for those who hear you."

Paul also instructed us in Titus 3:14:

> "Our people must also learn to engage in good deeds to meet pressing needs, so that they will not be unfruitful."

His reference to good deeds is the same as his reference to good works in previous Bible verses. We learn how to perform good works in and through our local church so we can bear fruit on Jesus' vine. We are taught how to perform our good works in our local church by individuals who know how to perform them.

KINGDOM OF GOD AND KINGDOM OF HEAVEN

The kingdom of God is a spiritual realm where God is everywhere present with His righteousness and holiness and where His rule is accepted and respected. The kingdom of heaven is in the kingdom of God. Only individuals on earth who have been redeemed by and reconciled to God through their faith and trust in and obedience to Jesus are received into the kingdom of God on earth while they are alive. All others on earth are separated from God because of sin. Loving, ministering to and serving others while we are alive because we love and obey Jesus ensure our entrance into the kingdom of heaven after we die (1 Timothy 4:14-16, 2 Peter 1:5-11).

The kingdom of heaven is a spiritual realm where God is present with His righteousness and holiness and where His rule is accepted and respected. The kingdom of heaven is separated from the earth because the earth has been corrupted by sin. God's angles are present there. The spirits and souls of individuals on earth who have been redeemed by and reconciled to God through Jesus before they die are present there. These include all those throughout the ages who have obediently responded to God's call and have done His will in their lives.

Jesus stated in Matthew 7:21-23:

> "Not everyone who says to Me, 'Lord, Lord,' will enter the kingdom of heaven, but he who does the will of My Father who is in heaven will enter. Many will say to Me on that day, 'Lord, did we not prophesy in Your name, and in Your name cast out demons, and in Your name perform many miracles?' And then I will declare to them, 'I never knew you; DEPART FROM ME, YOU WHO PRATICE LAWLESSNESS.'"

The Bible instructs us to spiritually grow and mature in our relationship with Jesus through the presence of the Holy Spirit in our life after we enter our relationship with Him. Paul stated in Ephesians 2:10 that we become "[God's] workmanship, created in Christ Jesus" to perform good works He prepares for us to perform when we enter this relationship. We perform our good works when we share God's love and grace with others, and we serve and minister to them in Jesus's name. We are to perform our good works for God's glory, not for our benefit nor to satisfy our personal needs. Jesus may not allow us to enter the kingdom of heaven after we die when we did not perform our good works for God's glory while we were alive, or when we have not repented of intentional sin in our life and asked Him to forgive us while we were alive.

MEANING OF THE TERMS KINGDOM OF GOD AND KINGDOM OF HEAVEN IN THE FOUR GOSPELS

Parables of Jesus in the Gospel of Matthew refer to the kingdom of heaven. The same parables in the other Gospels refer to the kingdom of God. This may be because the Gospel of Matthew was written for a Jewish audience while the other Gospels were written for non-Jewish audiences. Saying and writing the word for God is a sin for Jews. The use and meaning of the kingdom of heaven and the kingdom of God are the same in the four Gospels.

OLD TESTAMENT SUPERSCRIPTS

Many of the New Testament scriptures presented throughout this book have Old Testament superscript references embedded in them. These references identify the Old Testament sources for the texts contained in the scriptures.

Douglas D. Reynolds, Ph.D.

CHAPTER 1
INTRODUCTION

THIS BOOK

This is the fourth book in my *Redeemed by God* series. This book addresses:

- The eternal nature and sovereignty of God;
- Satan as the god of this world;
- The nature and character of sin and its relation to our spiritual death, rebirth and life;
- The functions of our soul and spirit;
- Our relationship with God and the redemption He extends to us through our faith and trust in and obedience to Jesus;
- God's requirements for us to grow and mature in our understanding of His word in the Bible and to engage in good works He prepares for us to perform;
- Jesus' judgments of the unrighteous at the great white throne judgment and of the righteous on the last day; and
- The new earth, heaven and Jerusalem God will create and the kingdom of heaven the righteous will inherit and enter.

ETERNAL NATURE OF GOD

God is *eternal*. He has no beginning and no ending. His existence is from everlasting to everlasting. He exists forever, and His judgments have eternal consequences. Jesus' judgments at the end of His 1,000- year kingdom will fix our position with God, Him and the Holy Spirit forever; it will never change.

    Eternity spans a period referred to as *infinity*. We can neither imagine nor comprehend a time span this long. Our life normally spans a period of 80 - 90 years. The age of the Universe is 13,800,000,000 years. *Infinity* is massively larger than the age of the Universe. Mathematically, any number divided by *infinity* equals *zero*. Therefore, our life span of 80 - 90 years represents a time span of *zero* years (e.g. 90/13,8000,000,000 = 0.0000000065 = 0) when compared to *infinity*.

Our life choices and actions during this *zero* time span determine where we will spend *eternity*. They determine whether we will forever be in the kingdom of heaven in the presence of God, Jesus and the Holy Spirit or whether we will forever be separated from Them in suffering and torment in the lake of fire.

MY RELATIONSHIP WITH GOD THROUGH JESUS

God has revealed Himself to me as I have read and studied the Bible. The Holy Spirit has helped me to better understand God's promises and spiritual life principles in the Bible as I have sought God and moved into a more intimate relationship with Him through Jesus. The Holy Spirit has shown me the Bible is truth as I have studied and internalized the Scriptures. God reveals Himself to us in the Bible. He presents His covenants and promises that He is faithful to keep and His spiritual life principles that govern our life in the Bible.

I found the process of accepting Jesus into my life as Lord and Savior was simple and straight forward when I became a Christian as a teenager in 1961. I understood the redemption and reconciliation God extended to me through Jesus were gifts. However, the process of surrendering control of the core area of my life to God, learning His spiritual life principles, and developing the knowledge, wisdom and faith to apply them to my life has been a demanding lifelong process. God has revealed Himself to me as I have studied His word in the Bible and trusted and yielded control of my life to Him. I have grown to know His love is real, and I can trust Him with every aspect of my life. I understand how He desires to work in and through my life through the Holy Spirit. He has given me the ability to live a spirit-filled life and to reach out to others in love to witness about the presence of Jesus in my life.

I discovered God loved and accepted me as I was when I entered my relationship with Him through Jesus. I did not have to change and become someone different to come into His presence. This was a major freeing revelation to me. We are deceived into believing we are not good enough to come into God's presence. We believe we must change and transform our own life before He will accept us. We would never be able to approach God if this were true because it is impossible for us to transform ourself independent of the presence of the Holy Spirit in our life. The Bible first teaches God loves and accepts us as we are - warts and all. It then teaches He loves us too much to allow us to stay who we are. The Holy Spirit enters our life and begins the process of renewing our mind and transforming our heart as we give Him permission, making us into the person God has created us to be.

I have learned I have intrinsic value in God's eyes as I have grown in my relationship with Him through Jesus over the years. I have worth and value in and of myself that is independent of anything I may or may not do for God or for others. I have worth and value that are independent of what others may think of or how they may choose to relate to me.

For that matter, the worth and value I have in God's eyes are independent of what I think of myself. I have learned I have worth and value solely because I am made in God's image. He wants His Spirit to dwell in me, and He has made an infinite sacrifice through His Son, Jesus, to redeem me and restore my broken relationship with Him. This understanding has been essential for the increased sense of healthy self-esteem and self-worth I have developed because of my relationship with God through Jesus.

God has never forced me to do anything I have not wanted to do. He has often been persistent in pursuing and leading me in directions He wanted me to go and in doing things He wanted me to do. However, the choices to obey or disobey Him have been mine. God has respected and accepted my choices even when they were contrary to what I perceived He wanted me to do. He has never complained, criticized or stopped loving me for making choices contrary to His will. However, He has never shielded or spared me from their consequences. One of the many mysteries of God's relationship with me is how He has been able to lead me in a positive and affirming manner to do those things He wanted me to do despite my initial refusals to do them.

ORTHODOX BELIEFS OF THE CHRISTIAN FAITH

Orthodox beliefs of the Christian faith define the nature and character of our relationship with God through His Son, Jesus. They are supported by the Bible and creed statements handed down to us by the early church fathers. These beliefs are:

- The Bible is the inspired word of God. It is God's primary method of communicating with us today. It has been given to us by men who were inspired and led by the Holy Spirit when they wrote it.

- God is Trinity. There are three eternal persons within the Godhead, but there is only one God. God is Father, Son, and Holy Spirit. The Father, Son, and Holy Spirit each possess all the infinite attributes of God and respond to us in a manner that is internally consistent with the nature and character of the Godhead. They respond to us as one God; however, they each relate to us in ways that are unique to Their respective positions within the Godhead.

- God the Father created heaven and earth and everything visible and invisible in them. Everyone on earth and in heaven is accountable to the Father.

- Jesus is the Son of God. He is the One through whom and for whom all things have been created and in whom all things in creation are held together.

- Jesus was conceived in Mary by the Holy Spirit. Mary, the mother of Jesus, was a virgin when Jesus was conceived in her womb.

- Jesus was in every way tempted as we are tempted, yet He resisted all temptations and led a life without sin.

- Jesus was crucified and died. He was buried. He was raised from the dead on the third day after His death. He ascended into heaven where He is now seated with God the Father. Jesus experienced a literal death and resurrection. We like Jesus will experience a literal death and resurrection.

- Jesus voluntarily accepted God's penalty of death for our sins. God accepted His death as a sufficient sacrifice for our sins when He died on a cross.

- The Holy Spirit is God in the world within us today. The Father and Son sent the Holy Spirit to make us aware of our sinful natures, to call us to repent for our sinful way of living, and to return to the Father through Jesus. The Holy Spirit opens our minds to receive and understand God's word in the Bible, and He intercedes to the Father on our behalf to make our needs and desires known to Him.

- The Church is the Body of Christ in the world today, and Jesus is its head.

- We are born into this world with a sin nature that separates us from God because of the original sin committed by Adam and Eve in the garden of Eden.

- We are redeemed by God's grace through our faith and trust in and obedience to Jesus. God forgives our sins, reconciles us to Himself, and receives us back into His presence when we repent of our sins and accept Jesus as our Lord and Savior.

- Jesus will return to earth and set up His 1,000-year kingdom at the end of the seven-year tribulation. The great white throne judgment will occur at the end of His kingdom. The existing earth and heaven will be destroyed, after which we will stand before the great white throne to be judged. Those whose names are written in the book of life will live throughout eternity with God, Jesus and the Holy Spirit in the new earth, heaven and Jerusalem God will create after this judgment. Those whose names are not written in the book of life will live throughout eternity separated from Them in the lake of fire.

- Those whose names are written in the book of life will stand before Jesus. He will examine the good works they have performed during their lives and what motivated them to perform them. Jesus will give them the reward they are to receive for performing their good works.

Knowledge of these orthodox beliefs of the Christian faith makes it easier for us to recognize misleading teachings within Christian churches and false doctrines associated with non-Christian cults. These cults often claim to be compatible with Christianity or falsely identify themselves as being Christian. However, they reject many or all the above orthodox beliefs. We can discern misleading teachings and false doctrines that are related to Christianity with greater certainty when we know and understand the underlying principles associated with these orthodox belie.

CONCLUDING COMMENTS

I do not consider myself to be a Bible scholar or an expert on Bible prophesy. I believe there are many others far more qualified to present the information I present in this book. However, the Holy Spirit has created a burden within my heart and presented me with the opportunity and means to write and publish this book. I believe He has given me an understanding of Bible scriptures and prophesies, has led me to relevant reference materials, and has given me the spiritual insight and vision necessary to write this book.

Whether you agree or disagree with my narratives and observations regarding our relationship with God through Jesus is not important. However, your ability and willingness to perceive and understand God is present and working in your life through the Holy Spirit is important. He desires to bring you into a reconciled relationship with Him through His Son, Jesus. You must understand and believe God is in control of events in your life that have, are and will occur in the future. He will walk with you to prepare your way as you encounter life's experiences and challenges when you invite Him into your life through Jesus and give Him permission through the Holy Spirit to work in and through you as you encounter these experiences and challenges.

CHAPTER 2
NATURES OF GOD AND SATAN

GOD - GOD OF GODS AND LORD OF LORDS

The Eternal Nature of God

God is *eternal*. The nature and attributes of His character have no beginning and no end, and they will never change. The Old Testament declares the eternal nature of God. In one of the earliest books of the Bible, Elihu, one of Job's companions, stated in Job 36:26:

> "Behold, God is exalted, and we do not know Him; the number of His years is unsearchable."

The Psalms declare the eternal nature of God.

> "Before the mountains were born or You gave birth to the earth and the world, even from everlasting to everlasting, You are God." (Psalms 90:2)

> "But the lovingkindness of the LORD is from everlasting to everlasting on those who fear Him, and His righteousness to children's children, to those who keep His covenant and remember His precepts to do them." (Psalm 103:17-18)

> "Forever, O LORD, Your word is settled in heaven. Your faithfulness continues throughout all generations; You established the earth, and it stands." (Psalms 119:89-90)

Isaiah stated in Isaiah 41:4:

> "Who has performed and accomplished it, calling forth the generations from the beginning? 'I, the LORD, am the first, and with the last. I am He.'"

The New Testament declares the eternal nature of God. Paul stated in Romans 1:20:

"For since the creation of the world His invisible attributes, His eternal power and divine nature, have been clearly seen, being understood through what has been made, so that they are without excuse."

Peter stated in 1 Peter 1:24:

"For 'all flesh is like grass, and all its glory like the flower of grass. The grass withers, and the flower falls off, but the word of the LORD endures forever.' (Isaiah 40:6-8)" (Note: *Superscript Bible references denote the Old Testament source for the preceding Scripture.*)

In Hebrews 1:8-12, the writer stated:

"But of the Son He says, 'Your throne, O God, is forever and ever,
And the righteous scepter is the scepter of His kingdom.
You have loved righteousness and hated lawlessness,
Therefore God, Your God, has anointed You
With the oil of gladness above Your companion.' Psalms 45:6-7
And
'You, LORD, in the beginning laid the foundation of the earth,
And the heavens are the work of Your hands;
They will perish, but You remain;
And they all will become old like a garment,
And like a mantle You will roll them up,
Like a garment they will also be changed.
But You are the same,
And Your years will not come to an end.' Psalm 102:25-27"

God, Jesus and the Holy Spirit have eternal natures. In Hebrews 13:8 the author also stated, "Jesus Christ is the same yesterday and today and forever."

The Old and New Testaments confirm the eternal natures of God and Jesus. The Bible indicates the words They spoke will stand forever. Psalms 119:89-90 above indicates God's word is settled in heaven forever. Isaiah stated in Isaiah 40:8:

"The grass withers, the flower fades, but the word of our God stands forever."

Peter reaffirmed God's word endures forever. Jesus stated in Matthew 5:17-19:

"Do not think that I came to abolish the Law or the Prophets; I did not come to abolish but to fulfill. For truly I say to you, until heaven and earth pass away, not the smallest letter or stroke shall pass from the Law until all is accomplished. Whoever then annuls one of the least of these commandments, and teaches others to do the same, shall be called least in the kingdom of heaven; but whoever keeps and teaches them, he shall be called great in the kingdom of heaven."

God's word is the eternal standard by which we must live our life and form our character. God's word and commandments stand forever and will never change. This contrasts with cultural and social customs and laws which continually change.

Solomon stated in Ecclesiastes 3:11:

"He has made everything appropriate in its time. He has also set eternity in their heart, yet so that man will not find out the work which God has done from the beginning even to the end."

God has placed eternity in our heart. This leads us to engage in life activities and make life choices that have eternal consequences. These actions often require us to look outside ourself to obtain information necessary to make correct choices. We as Christians approach God through Jesus and the Holy Spirit to obtain this information. We may not initially understand why and how God desires to work in and through us. However, God reveals Himself to us through the Holy Spirt to give us the information we seek as we grow in our knowledge of and internalize God's word in the Bible.

The Sovereignty and Power of God

Yahweh is the most important name for God in the Old Testament. It means *I am who I am*. The four-letter Hebrew word YHWH is the name by which God revealed Himself to Moses in the burning bush (Exodus 3:14). The name Yahweh expresses God is the infinite God, who is behind everything and to whom everyone in heaven and on earth is ultimately accountable. The *I am who I am* specifies nothing else defines who God is but God Himself.

The Bible teaches God has dominion over the earth and the heavens. In 1 Chronicles 29:11-12, the writer stated:

"Yours, O LORD, is the greatness and the power and the glory and the victory and the majesty, indeed everything that is in the heavens and the earth; Yours is the dominion, O LORD, and You exalt Yourself as head over all. Both riches and honor come from You, and You rule over all, and Your hand is power and might; and it lies in Your hand to make great and to strengthen everyone."

There is only one God even though there may be many so-called gods. God stated in Deuteronomy 32:39:

"See now that I, I am He, and there is no god besides Me; it is I who put to death and give life. I have wounded, and it is I who heal; and there is no one who can deliver from My hand."

Moses stated in Deuteronomy:

"To you it was shown that you might know that the LORD, He is God; there is no other besides Him. ... Know therefore today, and take it to your heart, that the LORD, He is God in heaven above and on earth below; there is no other." (Deuteronomy 4:35, 39)

"For the LORD your God is the God of gods and the LORD of lords, the great, the mighty, and the awesome God who does not show partiality, nor take a bribe." (Deuteronomy 10:17)

God stated in Isaiah 46:9:

"Remember the former things long past. For I am God, and there is no other; I am God, and there is no one like Me."

God is the Father of creation (Genesis 1:1, Revelation 4:11), Israel (Exodus 4:22-23, Jeremiah 31:9), Jesus (Matthew 3:16-17), and all who believe in Jesus (John 1:12-13, Romans 8:14).

The Spiritual Nature of God

God is a spiritual being. Jesus stated in John 4:24, "God is Spirit, and those who worship Him must worship in spirit and truth." As a spiritual being, God:

- Creates (Genesis 1:1)
- Destroys (Genesis 19:24-25)
- Provides (Psalm 104:27-30)
- Promotes (Psalm 75:6-7)
- Cares (1 Peter 5:6-7)

- Heals (Deuteronomy 32:39)
- Hears (Psalm 94:9-10)
- Hates (Proverbs 6:16)
- Grieves (Genesis 6:6)
- Loves (John 3:16)

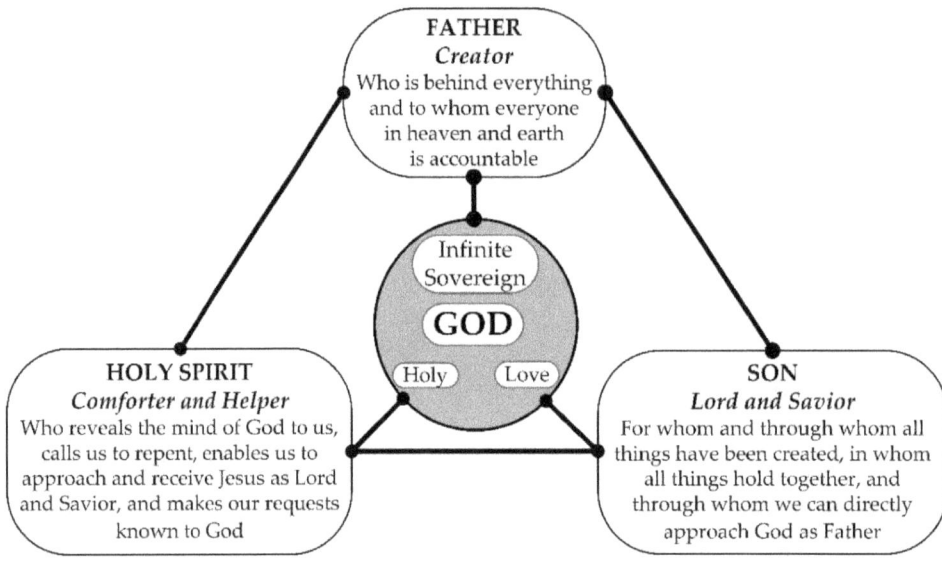

Figure 1

The Triune Nature of God

Even though there is one God, there are three eternal Persons within the Godhead who interact with each other and us. God is Father, Son and Holy Spirit (Figure 1). Each Person within the Godhead possesses all the eternal, infinite and sovereign attributes of Deity. They each interact with us in ways that are unique to their respective positions within the Godhead. However, they all interact with us in a unified manner that is perfectly consistent with God's sovereignty and His attributes of holiness and love. The Bible refers to:

- The Father as God (John 6:44-46, Romans 1:1-4, 1 Peter 1:2),
- Jesus, God's Son, as God (Matthew 14:32, Hebrews 1:1-3), and
- The Holy Spirit as God (Acts 2:16-18, Ezekiel 36:26-28).

Jesus stated in John 14:16-7:

> "And I will ask the Father, and He will give you another Helper, that He may be with you forever; that is the Spirit of Truth, whom the world cannot receive, because it does not behold Him or know Him, but you know Him because He abides with you, and will be in you."

He also stated in Matthew 28:19-20:

> "Go therefore and make disciples of all the nations, baptizing them in the name of the Father and the Son and the Holy Spirit, teaching them to observe all that I commanded you, and lo, I am with you always, even to the end of the age."

God, the Father, is the Creator of all things. He is the One who is behind everything and the one to whom everyone in all creation is accountable. Jesus, God's Son, is the One through and for whom all things have been created, in whom all things hold together, and through whom we can approach God, the Father. The Holy Spirit is our Comforter and Helper. He is our Advocate before the Father and the One who reveals the mind of God to us. He calls us to repentance, enables us to approach and receive Jesus as Lord and Savior, and makes our requests known to God. The Holy Spirit opens our minds to receive and understand God's word in the Bible.

The Bible teaches, even though the Father, Son and Holy Spirit are God, there is a hierarchy within the Godhead. Paul stated in 1 Corinthians 11:3 and 15:28:

> "But I want you to understand that Christ is the head of every man, and the man is the head of a woman, and God is the head of Christ. ... When all things are subjected to Him, then the Son Himself also will be subjected to the One who subjected all things to Him, that God may be all in all."

Jesus is God, but He was and is obedient to God, the Father. He stated in John 5:30, 6:38, 14:28:

> "I can do nothing on My own initiative. As I hear, I judge; and My judgment is just, because I do not seek My own will, but the will of Him who sent me. ... For I have come down from heaven, not to do My own will, but the will of Him who sent Me. ... If you loved Me, you would have rejoiced, because I go to the Father; for the Father is greater than I."

Jesus stated the Holy Spirit proceeds from the Father (John 15:26) and was sent by both the Father (John 14:6) and Him (John 15.26). The Holy Spirit was sent to glorify Jesus (John 16:14), bring to our remembrance all Jesus has taught us (John 14:26), and reveal the mind and thoughts of God as God wanted them revealed (1 Corinthians 2:11).

Relative to creation, Paul stated in 1 Corinthians 8:5-6:

> "For even if there are so-called gods whether in heaven or on earth, as indeed there are many gods and many lords, yet for us there is but one God, the Father, from whom are all things, and we exist for Him; and one Lord, Jesus Christ, by whom are all things, and we exist through Him."

All things come from God, the Father, through Jesus as Lord. We exist and live for God through Jesus. Paul continued in 1 Corinthians 12:3:

> "Therefore, I make known to you, that no one speaking by the Spirit of God says, 'Jesus is accursed'; and no one can say, 'Jesus is Lord,' except by the Holy Spirit."

In summary:

- We exist for the pleasure of God (the Father) through Jesus as our Lord;
- We can only come to God (the Father) through Jesus as our Savior; and
- The Holy Spirit enables us to approach Jesus as our Lord and Savior.

Character of God

Table 1 lists twenty-six attributes of God's character that are revealed in the Bible. These attributes are divided into three categories: God's infinite nature and sovereignty, His holiness and His love.

Table 1

GOD (FATHER, SON AND HOLY SPIRIT) IS:			
INFINITE	Sovereign	Self-existent	Self-sufficient
Eternal	Omnipresent	Omnipotent	Omniscient
Immutable	Inscrutable	Incomprehensible	Life
Holy	Wise	Righteous	Just
Truth	Light	Good	Impartial
Faithfull			
Love	Mercy	Gracious	Forgiving
Patient			

God's Infinite Nature and Sovereignty

God is infinite. God's stature, love, righteousness, truth, and all the other attributes of His character know no bounds. (1 Kings 8:27, 2 Chronicles 2,6, 6:18, Daniel 4:34-35)

God is sovereign. God exercises absolute authority over His creation. He does what He pleases and is accountable to no one. He makes His decisions and establishes the principles of His kingdom with assistance from no one. He acts in accordance with the other attributes of His character and never emphasizes one attribute at the expense of the others. For example, He never expresses love at the expense of justice, and He shows no partiality in expressing His love or in carrying out His justice. (Deuteronomy 32:39, Isaiah 40:10, 50:4-5, 61:1)

God is self-existent. God exists because He exists. He is not dependent on anything or anyone for His thoughts, will, power, or counsel. (Romans 11:33-34, Ephesians 1:5, Psalm 115:3, Psalm 33:10-11)

God is self-sufficient. God has never had in eternity past, nor can ever have in the future a need for which His divine nature has not already provided. (Psalm 50:10-12)

God is eternal. He has no beginning, and He will have no end. According to the Bible, His years are unsearchable, and He is from everlasting to everlasting. (Job 36:26, Psalm 90:2, Isaiah 40:8)

God is omniscient. God possesses all the knowledge and wisdom that ever has been or ever will be. He knows everything that has ever happened, is happening, or ever will happen. (Psalm 147:5, Hebrews 4:13)

God is omnipresent. God is everywhere present throughout all time and space. (Proverbs 15:3, Jeremiah 23:24, Hebrews 4:13)

God is omnipotent. God is all powerful and has the power and energy to do the sum of all things. (Daniel 4:34-35, Matthew 19:26)

God is immutable. His nature and attributes and His relationship with His creation never change. He will never call anything back once He has spoken it into existence; it stands forever. What God has spoken through the Bible in ancient times is true, valid and powerful today. (Isaiah 40:8, Malachi 3:6, Hebrews 13:8, James 1:17)

God is inscrutable. It is not possible to understand the inexplicable and mysterious ways of God. For example: Why does a loving and caring God allow certain terrible tragedies to occur? (Romans 11:33)

God is incomprehensible. It is not possible to probe the depths of God's mind and completely know and understand all His wisdom and knowledge. It is possible to know and understand only what God reveals to us through the Bible with the help of the Holy Spirit. (Ecclesiastes 3:11, Isaiah 55:8-9)

God is life. God is the only being who has life in and of Himself, and all life proceeds from Him. The Bible teaches it is possible to have true life only with the presence of God's indwelling Spirit. (Nehemiah 9:6, Job 33:4, Psalms 36:9, John 5:26)

God's Holiness

God is Holy. The most prominent attribute of God in the Bible is His holiness. Some suggest God's holiness is the attribute that ties all His other attributes together. God emphasizes His holiness by direct commands, objects, personal visions, and individual judgments. (Leviticus 19:2, Psalm 99:9, 1 Peter 1:15)

God is wise. God's wisdom is based on His omniscience. He can use His knowledge in a manner consistent with His holiness. (Psalm 136:5, 1 Timothy 1:17, Jude 1:25)

God is righteous. God will never do or cause anything that is wrong, evil or imperfect. He has and will never act in a malicious manner. He is the standard by which all moral and ethical standards are compared and judged. (Psalm 119:137, Psalm 145:17, John 7:18, Romans 3:26)

God is just. God will never do anything that is unfair in relation to any of His creation either in heaven or on earth. God executes His justice in accordance with His righteousness and is fair, even to those who stand in rebellion against Him. However, His righteousness demands He judge and expel from His presence all those in whom sin dwells. (Deuteronomy 32:4, Romans 3:26)

God is truth. All true knowledge and wisdom come only from God. Anything that opposes what God has revealed in the Bible is not truth. (2 Samuel 7:28, Isaiah 65:16, John 8:31-32)

God is light. God is the source and strength of all illumination. He is the source of all moral, mental and spiritual information and inspiration. (John 1:4-9, 1 Peter 2:9, 1 John 1:5-7, James 1:17)

God is good. This is the nature of God that disposes Him to be kind, cordial, benevolent and full of good will and compassion toward His creation and us. (Psalm 107:8, Romans 2:4)

God is impartial. God shows no partiality in measuring out His love or His justice. The standards of His righteousness apply equally to everyone. God does not establish one set of standards and laws for one group and a different set for another group. He treats everyone the same and shows no favors. All the attributes of His character apply equally to everyone. (Deuteronomy 10:17, Romans 2:11)

God is faithful. God can be trusted to keep His covenants and to follow through on the many promises He has given to us in the Bible. (Deuteronomy 7:9, 2 Timothy 2:13)

God's Love

God is love. God's love desires the temporal good and the eternal redemption of His creation. His love is extended in an unmerited fashion to everyone. It is given without any consideration of the merit or worth of those to whom it is extended. However, God loves us in a manner that is consistent with His holiness. His love for us will not violate the attributes of His righteousness and justice. (Romans 5:8, 1 John 4:16)

God is merciful. God's mercy seeks the temporal good in the earthly existence and the eternal salvation of all who have opposed His will, even at the cost of infinite self-sacrifice. Mercy is the aspect of God's love that causes Him to help those who either because of sin or of circumstances beyond their control have special needs. This help is selective in nature and undeserved. Mercy is the aspect of God's love that predisposes Him to withhold deserved punishment associated with sin. (Exodus 34:6, Psalm 103:8-17, 1 Timothy 1:13-16)

God is gracious. God's grace seeks to show undeserved favor and bestow undeserved position without regard to the merit or worth of those to whom it is extended and who receive it. Grace is the aspect of God's love that predisposes Him to redeem and reconcile us to Himself through the death and resurrection of His Son, Jesus. (Romans 3:24, Ephesians 2:8-9)

God is forgiving. Forgiveness is that aspect of God's love in which His mercy and grace are brought together through Jesus' shed blood on a cross. God forgives our sins, reconciles us to Himself, and adopts us back into His kingdom through Jesus' death and resurrection. (Matthew 9:2-5, Hebrews 10:17-22, James 5:15, 1 John 9:2-5)

God is patient. Patience is the aspect of God's love that predisposes Him to endure the actions of those in whom sin dwells and withhold deserved eternal judgment. God is patient in His efforts to lead people to repentance. However, His attributes of righteousness and justice will ultimately lead Him to judge and eternally punish all in whom sin dwells and who do not repent and receive the gifts of His grace and redemption extended to them through Jesus. (Exodus 34:6, Romans 2:4, 2 Peter 3:9, 15, 2 Thessalonians 1:5-10)

The Laws of God

God has given us laws that direct how we are to relate to Him and interact with others. The Bible refers to these laws as the Law of Moses. The Ten Commandments Moses received from God on Mount Sinai form the core of His laws that cover our relationships with Him and our parents and our interactions with others. They are (Deuteronomy 5:7-21):

- "You shall have no other gods before Me."
- You shall not make for yourself an idol, or any likeness of what is in heaven above on the earth beneath or in the water under the earth. You shall not worship them or serve them; for I, the LORD your God, am a jealous God, visiting the iniquity of the fathers on the children, and on the third and the fourth generations of those who hate Me, but showing loving kindness to thousands, to those who love Me and keep My commandments.
- "You shall not take the name of the LORD your God in vain, for the LORD will not leave him unpunished who takes His name in vain."
- "Observe the Sabbath day to keep it holy, as the LORD your God commanded you. Six days you shall labor and do all your work, but the seventh day is a Sabbath of the LORD your God; in it you shall not do any work, you or your son or your daughter or your male servant or your female servant or your ox or your donkey or any of your cattle or your sojourner who stays with you, so that your male servant and your female servant may rest as well as you."
- "Honor your father and your mother, as the LORD your God has commanded you, that your days may be prolonged, and that it may go well with you on the land which the LORD your God gives you.

- "You shall not murder."
- "You shall not commit adultery."
- "You shall not steal."
- "You shall not bear false witness against your neighbor."
- "You shall not covet your neighbor's wife, and you shall not desire your neighbor's house, his field or his male servant or his female servant, his ox or his donkey or anything that belongs to your neighbor."

Old Testament laws received by Moses in addition to the Ten Commandments are treated as extensions of the Ten Commandments. The Ten Commandments plus these laws form what is referred to as the Law. Jesus indicated in Matthew 5:18 that "not the smallest letter or stroke" shall be removed from the Law until heaven and earth pass away. Therefore, the Law defines and convicts us of sin.

Sexual sins associated with the commandment on adultery include:

- **Adultery (**Leviticus 20:10; Deuteronomy 22:13-22): Adultery is sexual contact between a man and woman, one or both who are married, but not to each other.
- **Fornicatio**n (Exodus 22:16-17; Deuteronomy 22:20-30): Fornication is sexual contact between a man and woman neither of whom is married nor engaged to be married. A man and woman engaged to be married are not to have sexual contact until after they are married.
- **Homosexuality** (Leviticus 18:22, 20:13): Homosexuality is sexual contact between men and women of the same gender.
- **Incest** (Leviticus 20:11-12, 14; Deuteronomy 27:20, 22-23): Incest is sexual contact between parents and children of opposite gender, between brothers and sisters, and between aunts, uncles, nieces, nephews and cousins of opposite gender.
- **Bestiality** (Exodus 22:20; Leviticus 18:23, 20:15-16): Bestiality is sexual contact between a man or woman and an animal.
- **Exposing of Nakedness** (Leviticus 18:8-17, 20:17): Exposing of nakedness in a family is looking at the nude body of a family member of different gender other than a spouse. This includes viewing modern-day pornography.

Sin in our life creates a barrier that separates us from God. The Bible teaches the Law cannot remove this barrier and redeem us from sin. It can only convict us of sin and condemn us to spiritual death and eternal separation from God, Jesus and the Holy Spirit.

SATAN - GOD OF THIS WORLD

There are many who doubt the existence of Satan. They may believe there is something or someone who is a personification of evil in the world, but they do not believe there is a real spiritual being named Satan. The Bible clearly teaches Satan's existence (Ron Rhodes, *Angels Among Us*, 1994). He is mentioned in seven Old Testament books: Genesis, 1 Chronicles, Job, Psalms, Isaiah, Ezekiel, and Zechariah. He is mentioned in nineteen of the twenty-seven books in the New Testament. He is mentioned by every New Testament writer:

- Matthew (Matthew 4:1)
- Mark (Mark 5:15)
- Luke (Luke 22:3)
- John (1 John 3:8)
- Paul (Romans 16:20)
- Peter (1 Peter 5:8)
- James (James 4:7)
- Jude (Jude 9)

He is mentioned by Jesus some twenty-five times in the Gospels. References are found in Matthew 4:10, Matthew 16:23, Matthew 25:41, Luke 10:18, John 8:44, and Luke 22:31. To deny the existence of Satan is to deny the validity of statements concerning his existence in the Bible and Jesus' own testimony.

God created three angels who had special positions. One was Michael, referred to as an archangel (Daniel 10:13, Jude 1:9). Another was Gabriel, identified as a special messenger angel from the very presence of God (Daniel 9:21, Luke 1:19). The third was Lucifer, who some Bible scholars believe was given the special task of watching over the throne of God. Ezekiel described Lucifer, the son of dawn, in Ezekiel 28:12-17:

> "Again the word of the LORD came to me saying, 'Son of man, take up a lamentation over the king of Tyre, and say to him, 'Thus says the LORD God, you had the seal of perfection, full of wisdom and perfect in beauty. You were in Eden, the garden of God; every precious stone was your covering; the ruby, the topaz, and the diamond; the beryl, the onyx, and the jasper; the lapis lazuli, the turquoise, and the emerald; and the gold, the workmanship of your settings and sockets, was in you. On the day that you were created they were prepared. You were the anointed cherub who covers, and I placed you there. You were on the holy mountain of God; you walked in the midst of the stones of fire. You were blameless in your ways from the day you were created, until unrighteousness was found in you. By the abundance of your trade you were internally filled with violence, and you sinned; therefore I have cast you as profane from the mountain of God.

And I have destroyed you, O covering Cherub, from the midst of the stones of fire. Your heart was lifted up because of your beauty; you corrupted your wisdom by reason of your splendor. I cast you to the ground; I put you before kings, that they may see you.'"

According to this description, Lucifer was perhaps the most beautiful creature in heaven. He was the anointed cherub. A cherub is a special angelic being who magnifies the holiness and power of God and serves as a visible reminder of the majesty and glory of God and His abiding presence with His people. Some Bible scholars speculate Lucifer led the worship in heaven and had the special task of watching over the throne of God. However, pride entered his heart because of his beauty and position. He no longer wanted to worship and serve God; he wanted to be served and worshiped. Isaiah implied this in Isaiah 14:12-15:

"How you have fallen from heaven, O star of the morning, son of the dawn! You have been cut down to the earth, you who have weakened the nations! But you said in your heart, 'I will ascend to heaven; I will raise my throne above the stars of God, and I will sit on the mount of assembly in the recess of the north. I will ascend above the heights of the clouds; I will make myself like the Most High.' Nevertheless you will be thrust down to Sheol, to the recesses of the pit."

Many of the angels in heaven rebelled against God with him. Lucifer and those angels who followed him were defeated and cast out of heaven. Jesus implied this when He stated in Luke 10:18, "I was watching Satan fall from heaven like lightning."

Lucifer's name was changed to Satan when he was cast out of heaven. A name change in the Bible usually denotes a corresponding change in relationship with God. Abram became Abraham. Sarai became Sarah. Jacob became Israel. Simon became Peter, and Saul became Paul. These name changes implied moving into a more favored and closer relationship with God. Satan's name changes corresponded to his moving into a relationship more removed from God and his resulting judgment.

Satan is a fallen angel who was corrupted by sin. He is a created being (Ezekiel 28:12-17). Even though he possesses great power, he does not possess any of the sovereign and infinite attributes of God. Like all other created beings, his powers are limited by God.

The Bible teaches Satan is the god of this world (2 Corinthians 4:3-4) and the world is under his control (1 John 5:10). When Jesus was tempted by Satan after His forty days in the wilderness, the following account is given in Matthew 4:8-9:

"Again the devil took Him to a very high mountain and showed Him all the kingdoms of the world, and their glory; and he said to Him, 'All these things will I give You, if You fall down and worship me.' Then Jesus said to him, 'Be gone, Satan! For it is written, 'You shall worship the LORD Your God, and serve Him only.'" (Deuteronomy 6:13)"

Jesus did not dispute Satan's claim to dominion over the kingdoms of the world, but He rebuked and commanded him to depart. Satan is a trespasser who has dominion because men and women whose hearts have been darkened and blighted by sin have given it to him. He rules over the world today because men and women choose to follow and serve him instead of God. Regarding this, Jesus stated in John 8:41-44:

"They said to Him, 'We were not born of fornication; we have one Father, God.' Jesus said to them, 'If God were your Father, you would love Me, for I proceeded forth and have come from God, for I have not even come on My own initiative, but He sent Me. Why do you not understand what I am saying? It is because you cannot hear My word. You are of your father the devil, and you want to do the desires of your father. He was a murderer from the beginning, and does not stand in the truth, because there is no truth in him. Whenever he speaks a lie, he speaks from his own nature, for he is a liar, and the father of lies.'"

Satan works to undermine the works of God, destroy His kingdom, deny Him possession of those things that are rightfully His, and imitates God. He has:

- A false trinity (Revelation 16:13),
- Synagogues (Revelation 2:9),
- Doctrines (1 Timothy 4:1-3),
- Mysteries (Revelation 2:24, 2 Thessalonians 2:7),
- A throne (Revelation 2:13),
- A kingdom (Luke 4:5-6),
- Worshipers (Revelation 13:4),
- Fallen angels (Revelation 12:7-8),
- Ministers (2 Corinthians 11:15),
- Miracles (2 Thessalonians 2:9-10),

- Sacrifices and fellowship (1 Corinthians 10:19-21), and
- Armies (Revelation 19:19).

In addition to imitating God, Satan:

- Sows tares among God's wheat (Matthew 13:24-30, 36-43);
- Instigates false doctrines (1 Timothy 4:1-3);
- Perverts God's word (Genesis 3:1-4, Matthew 4:6);
- Hinders the works of God's servants (1 Thessalonians 2:18);
- Resists the prayers of God's servants (Daniel 10:12-13);
- Blinds individuals to the truth (2 Corinthians 4:4);
- Steals God's word from human hearts (Matthew 13:19);
- Accuses Christians before God (Job 1:7-12, 2:3-6, Zechariah 3:1-4);
- Lays snares for individuals (2 Timothy 2:26);
- Tempts (Matthew 4:1, Ephesians 6:11);
- Afflicts (Job 2:7, Acts 10:38);
- Deceives (Revelations 12:9);
- Undermines the sanctity of the home (1 Corinthians 7:3-5); and
- Prompts both Christians and non-Christians to transgress against the holiness of God (1 Chronicles 21:1, John 13:2, Matthew 16:22-23, Acts 5:3).

God did not initially want Satan to have dominion over the earth. However, He allowed Satan to seize dominion because of Adam's and Eve's disobedience. They were originally given dominion over the earth (Genesis 1:28). Therefore, only a perfect man without sin, Jesus, could pay the required ransom to regain dominion from Satan (Matthew 20:28, 1 Timothy 2:6, Hebrews 9:15).

Jesus stated Satan is a murderer and liar; he is a thief who comes to kill, steal and destroy (John 8:44, 10:10). Peter stated in 1 Peter 5:8:

> "Be of sober spirit, be on the alert. Your adversary, the devil, prowls about like a roaring lion, seeking someone to devour."

John indicated in 1 John 3:8, "The one who practices sin is the devil; for the devil has sinned from the beginning." Satan is a liar and master of deception. Paul indicated he is an angel of light who disguises himself to lure people away from God (2 Corinthians 11:14-15), and he works to put a veil over "the minds of the unbelieving, that they might not see the light of the gospel of the glory of Christ" (2 Corinthians 4:3-4).

The Bible teaches Satan has been judged and defeated through the death and resurrection of Jesus (John 12:21, John 16:11, 1 John 3:8). He has a lake of fire waiting for him (Revelation 20:10). Dominion is returned to us when God and Jesus take up residence in us through the Holy Spirit (Acts 26:16-18, Colossians 1:13). We then have authority in the name of Jesus over Satan, and he must obey. John stated 1 John 4:4:

> "You are from God little children, and have overcome them; because greater is He who is in you than he who is in the world."

James indicated in James 4:2, "Submit therefore to God. Resist the devil and he will flee from you."

DOMINION VERSUS OWNERSHIP

God has ultimate dominion over and ownership of the heavens and earth. Ezra stated 1 Chronicles 29:11-12:

> "Thine, O LORD, is the greatness and the power and the glory and the victory and the majesty, indeed everything that is in the heavens and the earth; Thine is the dominion, O LORD, and Thou dost exalt Thyself as head over all. Both riches and honor come from Thee, and Thou dost rule over all, and in Thy hand is power and might; and it lies in Thy hand to make great, and to strengthen everyone."

David stated in Psalm 24:1:

> "The earth is the LORD's, and all it contains, the world, and those who dwell in it."

The LORD stated in Deuteronomy 10:14:

> "Behold, to the LORD your God belongs heaven and the highest heavens, the earth and all that is in it."

Leviticus 25:23 teaches God owns all land. Haggai 2:8 states God owns all gold and silver. Psalm 50:10-12 indicates all livestock belongs to God. The Bible teaches God is the creator and owner of all things in heaven and on earth. He did not transfer ownership even though He originally transferred dominion of His creation on earth to Adam. Therefore, Adam did not have the authority to transfer ownership even though he transferred dominion over the earth to Satan because of sin. Only God has this authority, and He has not given it to either man or Satan.

Dualism is often taught when addressing the conflict between God and Satan. It presumes God and Satan are equal: God representing good and Satan representing evil. The conflict between good and evil in the world is then portrayed as a conflict between God and Satan who are equally powerful. The Bible does not support this. Satan is an angelic being who was originally created to watch over the throne of God. He was cast out of heaven because of sin. His powers are defined and limited by God. The book of Job in the Old Testament indicates the pain and suffering with which Satan was allowed to afflict Job were limited by God. God has placed boundaries on what Satan can and cannot do to us.

We are influenced by Satan when we reject God and ignore His lordship over our life. Sin as a result reigns in our life, and Satan can exercise dominion over us. Satan has become the god of this world and claimed dominion over it because mankind has rejected God's lordship over His creation. God has placed boundaries on the dominion he can exercise. The earth belongs to God even though Satan has been given dominion over it because of sin. Everything that happens in heaven and on earth occurs in a manner consistent with God's physical and spiritual laws.

CHAPTER 3
NATURE AND CHARACTER OF SIN

DEFINITION OF SIN

There are two Greek words that can be used to define sin: *parabasis*, which means to overstep a forbidden line, and *hamartano*, which means to miss the mark. John stated in 1 John 3:4

> "Everyone who practices sin also practices lawlessness; and sin is lawlessness."

Paul stated in Romans 3:23, "For all have sinned and fall short of the glory of God." We sin when we disobey God's laws. We step over lines of acceptable behavior established by God into areas of behavior forbidden by Him when we sin. We miss the mark when we sin; we do not achieve the level of perfection necessary to enter God's presence to fellowship and commune with Him. We are all guilty of sin. As a result, we are separated from God in the absence of a Savior who can restore this relationship.

ORIGIN OF SIN

Let us first examine the origin of sin in the universe. Biblical references in Ezekiel 28:11-19, Isaiah 14:12-15, Luke 10:18, 1 John 3:8, and Revelation 12:3-4 imply there was a revolt against God in heaven before creation that was led by Lucifer. This revolt is described in Ezekiel 28:11-19, Isaiah 14:12-15, and Revelation 12:3-4. The revolt was initiated when pride entered Lucifer, and he attempted to become like God. The Bible implies this revolt introduced sin into God's creation even though it failed, and Lucifer was cast out of heaven.

The Bible teaches sin originated because of the disobedience of Adam and Eve. God stated they could eat any of the fruit in the garden except the fruit on the tree of the knowledge of good and evil when He created and placed them in the Garden of Eden. He indicated the moment they ate this fruit they would die (Genesis 1:26-30, 2:7-25). The account of the fall of Adam and Eve is presented in Genesis 3:1-7:

"Now the serpent was more crafty than any beast of the field which the LORD God had made. And he said to the woman, 'Indeed, has God said, 'You shall not eat from any tree of the garden?' And the woman said to the serpent, 'From the fruit of the trees of the garden we may eat; but from the fruit of the tree which is in the middle of the garden, God has said, 'You shall not eat from it or touch it, lest you die.' And the serpent said to the woman, 'You surely shall not die; for God knows that in the day you eat from it your eyes will be opened, and you will be like God, knowing good and evil.' When the woman saw that the tree was good for food, and that it was a delight to the eyes, and that the tree was desirable to make one wise, she took from its fruit and ate; and she gave also to her husband with her, and he ate. Then the eyes of both of them were opened, and they knew that they were naked; and they sewed fig leaves together and made loin coverings."

This account implies Eve was deceived by the serpent. It also implies Adam was with her when she ate the forbidden fruit. God had given Adam and Eve dominion over all creatures on the earth, which included the serpent. Adam or Eve could have rebuked the serpent, and Satan who was a trespasser and had no legal authority or dominion on earth would have had to leave. However, they did not do this. They instead disobeyed God and ate the forbidden fruit.

Sin can be defined as **a deliberate act of disobeying God's commandments based on deception.** Adam and Eve chose to disobey God because they did not believe He would hold them accountable and discipline them for their disobedience. This is the basis for our rejection of God's word today. We deliberately choose to ignore God and disobey His commandments because we do not believe He will hold us accountable for our acts of disobedience.

GOD'S RESPONSE TO SIN

God's response to Adam's and Eve's disobedience is recorded in Genesis 3:14-19:

"And the LORD God said to the serpent, 'Because you have done this, cursed are you more than all cattle, and more than every beast of the field; on your belly shall you go, and dust shall you eat all the days of your life; and I will put enmity between you and the woman, and between your seed and her seed; he shall bruise you on the head, and you shall bruise him on the heel.' To the woman He said, 'I will greatly multiply your pain in child birth, in pain you shall bring forth children; yet your desire shall be for your husband, and he shall rule over you.' Then to Adam He said, 'Because you have listened to the voice of your wife, and have eaten from the tree about which I commanded you, saying,

'You shall not eat from it;' cursed is the ground because of you; in toil you shall eat of it all the days of your life. Both thorns and thistles it shall grow for you; and you shall eat the plants of the field; by the sweat of your face you shall eat bread, till you return to the ground, because from it you were taken; for you are dust, and to it you shall return.'"

God's response to the introduction of sin into His creation was:

To Lucifer: He was cast out of heaven and became Satan. God told him he would be judged. This judgment occurred when Jesus shed His blood and died on a cross and was raised from the dead.

To men and women: Spiritual and physical death, pain and suffering entered the world when Adam and Eve sinned. The Genesis account of creation implies God originally created men and women to live forever in fellowship with Him. He breathed His Spirit into Adam and Eve, which enabled them to fellowship with Him, when He created them. God withdrew His Spirit from them when they sinned, and they spiritually died. As a result, they were no longer able to fellowship with God. Consequently, all men and women have been and are born into this world spiritually dead. God's Spirit does not dwell in them. God also told Adam and Eve they would physically die. God provided for their needs before they sinned, but they had to provide for their own needs after fellowship with Him was broken. This has been the case for all men and women since Adam and Eve. God initially shielded Adam and Eve from pain and suffering, but He indicated they and all men and women after them would experience pain and suffering.

To nature: God created the earth a paradise where everything was in perfect harmony. The harmony was destroyed, and the paradise became a wilderness because of sin. The ground brought forth in abundance before sin entered the world. The ground brought forth weeds, thorns, thistles and barrenness in addition to the abundance it initially brought forth after sin entered the world.

CONSEQUENCES OF SIN

Sin has individual, social and cultural consequences. The individual consequences of sin include:

Sin dooms our soul (Ezekiel 18:4). It separates us from God. As a result, God's Spirit does not dwell in us, we are spiritually dead, and our spirit and soul are not nurtured and supported by God.

Sin devours our intellect (1 Corinthians 2:14, Romans 8:5-8). We are unable to receive and understand the spiritual life principles of God gives to us in the Bible when His Spirit does not dwell in us and nurture our spirit. As a result, our mind becomes controlled by the desires and teachings of the world, and we become hostile toward God.

Sin deceives and perverts our heart (Jeremiah 17:9, Mark 7:21-22). It causes evil thoughts, fornications, thefts, murders, adulteries, deeds of coveting and wickedness, deceit, sensuality, envy, slander, pride and foolishness to proceed from our heart.

Sin dulls our ears (Acts 28:27). It prevents us from hearing God's word when it is shared with us by others, and it prevents us from hearing God's voice when He quietly speaks to us through our spirit.

Sin darkens our eyes (Ephesians 4:18). It causes our soul to become darkened and blighted. We, therefore, are unable to experience God working in our individual life and see Him working in the lives of others and the world.

Sin diverts our feet (Isaiah 53:6). Sin causes us to rebel against God and entices us to do things that are offensive to Him and violate His commandments.

Sin defiles our tongue (Romans 3:13-14). Our mouth often speaks forth things that are unclean, profane and offensive to God because of sin, and it defiles our whole body.

Sin has created a chasm that separates us from God. Sin prevents us from entering a relationship with Him. His light does not shine in our heart because of sin. Consequently, our heart becomes blighted and dark. Sin deceives us into believing we have freedom to do anything we desire when in fact this freedom leads to bondage and causes our joy to turn to sorrow and our peace to be replaced with turmoil. Sin leads us into activities that destroy lives and relationships and cause pain and suffering. Sin destroys our positive self-image and takes away from us the confidence God wants us to have in our ability to do the things He wants us to do. Sin takes us farther into disobedient acts than we initially plan to go, causes us to stay involved in them longer than we initially want to stay, and costs us more in terms of guilt, shame, pain and suffering than we initially expect to have to pay.

Sin has caused a fallenness to permeate God's original creation. He initially created everything to be perfect and in perfect harmony. However, sin has caused everything to become corrupt and imperfect. There are flaws in everything. These flaws are universal across time and human experiences and have caused disruptions in the harmony of God's original creation.

The fallenness of creation because of sin brings with it the potential for evil. Evil originated from Satan's rebellion against God in heaven and Adam and Eve disobeying God in the Garden of Eden. Evil lurks in the shadows and background of natural events and human affairs, looking for the right opportunities to spring forth. Evil is associated with actions and activities that give rise to sin and result in negative and hurtful consequences. Evil results in destruction through natural and man- made events and causes harm, injury and death. Evil perpetuates itself through the fallenness of creation and the fallen nature of people.

CHAPTER 4
SPIRITUAL DEATH, REBIRTH AND LIFE

UNDERSTANDING OUR CONDITION

Genesis 1 - 3 provides insight into our original relationship with God. Moses indicated God first created the heavens and earth. He then created a man and woman in His own image and likeness and placed them in the Garden of Eden. God breathed life into them, and they became living beings. The man's name was Adam, and the woman's name was Eve. Adam and Eve were the crown of God's creation. Everything in God's creation was in perfect harmony. Adam and Eve lived in harmony with God, each other and the environment around them. This harmony was contingent on their obedience to God and living within behavioral boundaries He established. There were no death, disease, discord and disasters in God's original creation, and there were no guilt, shame, pain and suffering. God commanded Adam and Eve to:

- Exercise dominion over the earth (Genesis 1:26);
- Be fruitful and multiply by bearing children, fill and subdue the earth, and rule over every living creature (Genesis 1:28);
- Dress, till and take care of the garden of Eden (Genesis 2:15); and
- Not eat the fruit from the tree of knowledge of good and evil in the garden of Eden (Genesis 2:17).

God placed His Spirit in Adam and Eve when He created them. They were spiritually alive because God's Spirit was present in them. God walked and communed with them daily in the garden of Eden (Genesis 3:8). He gave them freedom to choose how they would interact with Him, each other and the environment where He placed them (Genesis 2:16). However, He commanded them to live within the behavioral boundaries He established (Genesis 2:18).

Satan deceived Adam and Eve into believing they would become like God, knowing good and evil, when they ate the fruit from the tree of knowledge of good and evil (Genesis 3:1-7).

Sin entered God's creation with their disobedience, and the harmony He established in His creation was destroyed. God withdrew His Spirit from Adam and Eve, and they spiritually died. Everyone since them has been and is born into this world spiritually dead because God's Spirit is not present in them. As a result, the minds and hearts of men and women have become hostile toward God without the intervention of Jesus. God placed a curse on Adam and Eve, the serpent and the earth because of their disobedience (Genesis 3:14-19). Sin caused spiritual and physical death, disease, discord and disasters to enter the world, and guilt, shame, pain and suffering entered the world with sin.

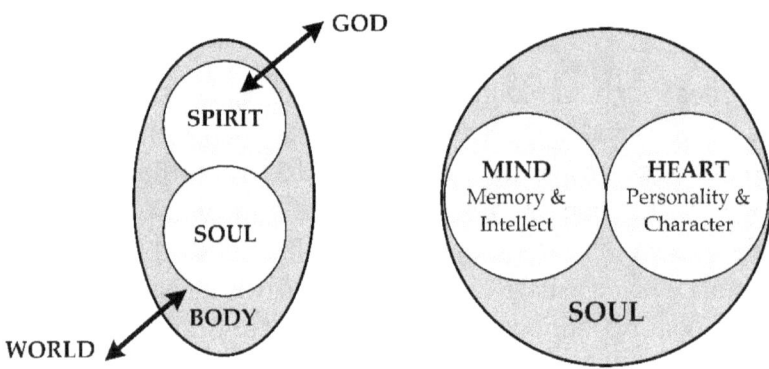

Figure 2

The consequences of Adam's and Eve's disobedience can be understood in terms of the nature of their and our creation. God created them with a spirit, soul and body (Figure 2). Moses stated in Genesis 2:7:

> "Then the LORD God formed man of dust from the ground, and breathed into his nostrils the breath of life; and man became a living being."

God formed Adam's body from the dust of the ground and breathed the breath of life into him. Adam was spiritually alive because God's Spirit was placed in him. Paul stated in 1 Thessalonians 5:23:

> "Now may the God of peace Himself sanctify you entirely; and may your spirit and soul and body be preserved complete, without blame at the coming of our Lord Jesus Christ."

He affirmed we are born with a spirit, soul and body. Adam and Eve interacted with their environment through their physical senses of sight, hearing, touch, smell and taste, and they interacted and communed with God in the spiritual realm through their spirit (Figure 2).

James stated in James 2:26 "the body without the spirit is dead." Our spirit resides in and functions through our body. It gives life to our body. Our spirit and soul function in and through our body while we are alive. They leave our body when it can no longer support physical life, and we die. Our body decays and returns to dust. Our spirit and soul continue in an eternal existence beyond death. They continue in the presence of God, Jesus and the Holy Spirit in the kingdom of heaven when we have been redeemed by and reconciled to God through Jesus. Our spirit and soul are separated from Them in Hades and eventually in the lake of fire when we have not sought and received the redemption and salvation God extends to us through Jesus.

Our soul and spirit have distinct functions. However, they are integrally linked. Jesus stated in Matthew 22:37-40:

> "'You shall love the Lord your God with all your heart, and with all your soul, and with all your mind.' (Deuteronomy 6:5) This is the great and foremost commandment. The second is like it, 'You shall love your neighbor as yourself.' (Leviticus 19:18) On these two commandments depend the whole Law and the Prophets."

His statement implied our soul is comprised of our mind and heart (Figure 5). Paul stated in 1 Corinthians 14:15:

> "What is the outcome then? I will pray with the spirit and I will pray with the mind also; I will sing with the spirit and I will sing with the mind also."

His statement implied our soul and spirit have distinct functions. God has created us with a body, spirit and soul. Our spirit resides in and functions through our body and gives it life. Our soul is linked with our spirit, and it controls the functions and actions of our body and spirit. **Our spirit is a body that resides in and gives life to our physical body. Our soul functions through our physical and spiritual bodies to enable us to interact with the physical world and the spiritual realm**.

Our soul is comprised of our mind and heart. Our mind is the seat of memory and intellect. Our memory is the repository of information and experiences we have processed and assimilated throughout our life. Our intellect is the knowledge and wisdom we have obtained from this information and these experiences. Our heart is the seat of our personality and character. Our personality is the organized pattern of behavioral characteristics that identify and define who we are. Our character defines the moral and ethical qualities of our personality.

Our soul controls the actions of our spirit and body. It is formed as we experience spiritual and physical life. It develops as it receives, processes and assimilates information from our spirit as we interact with God in the spiritual realm and from our five physical senses as we interact with the physical world. **Our soul develops and grows as our mind and heart process and assimilate information they receive from our life experiences. It controls how we encounter, interpret and respond to new life experiences based on how it has processed and assimilated information it has received from prior life experiences**.

Our spirit, soul and body develop as we encounter life. Our body develops and matures as we physically grow. It is the vessel through which our spirit interacts with God, others and the physical world. Our spirit and soul become the source and center of our conscience, insight and sensitivity and our creativity, inspiration and motivation as we spiritually and emotionally grow and mature.

Adam and Eve were spiritually alive before they disobeyed God and sinned. God's Spirit dwelt in them, and they fellowshipped with and were nurtured by His Spirit. Jesus stated in John 6:63:

> "It is the Spirit who gives life; the flesh profits nothing; the words that I have spoken to you are spirit and are life."

He affirmed God gave Adam and Eve spiritual life. God gives us spiritual life through Jesus and the Holy Spirit. We are spiritually alive when God's Spirit through the Holy Spirit dwells in us. Our soul is provided with the knowledge, wisdom and ability to bring our spirit and body into submission to the sovereign will and laws of God through the presence of the Holy Spirit. Our personality and character then develop in a manner pleasing to God, and they create within us the desire to live within the behavioral boundaries He has established.

SPIRITUAL DEATH

Adam and Eve were separated from and no longer able to commune with God when they disobeyed Him and sinned. God withdrew His Spirit from them, and they spiritually died (Figure 3). Spiritual death, which is associated with the absence of God's Spirit in our life, entered the world with sin.

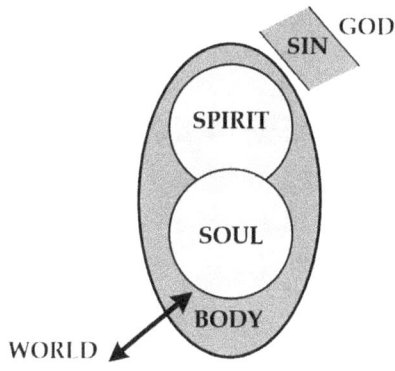

Figure 3

Everyone who has been born since Adam and Eve has been born without God's Spirit. We have been born into this world spiritually dead. We have rejected God even though He reveals Himself to us in His creation. Our minds and hearts have become blighted and darkened as a result.

Our spirit and soul are not nurtured by God's Spirit through the Holy Spirit when we are spiritually dead. our soul does not receive the spiritual knowledge, wisdom and strength from the Holy Spirit necessary to equip us to live according to God's spiritual life principles and laws. We receive information only from the environment where we live and the world. Our mind and heart become controlled by the desires of our flesh and what the worlds teaches us is truth. John stated in 1 John 2:15-16:

> "Do not love the world, nor the things in the world. If anyone loves the world, the love of the Father is not in him. For all that is in the world, the lust of the flesh and the lust of the eyes and the boastful pride of life, is not from the Father, but is from the world."

He indicated the thoughts and desires of our mind and heart when God's Spirit through the Holy Spirit does not live within us are controlled by:

- What we see and perceive with our eyes;
- What we perceive is necessary to satisfy the needs and cravings of our body; and
- Our pride and desire to control our life.

These cause us to transgress God's behavioral boundaries and laws and make us hostile toward Him. This is our condition without Jesus.

Spiritual death has current and eternal consequences. We are separated from God when we are spiritually dead. This separation becomes an eternal separation when we physically die before we can be redeemed by and reconciled to God through our faith in Jesus. In Hebrews 9:27, the author stated, "And inasmuch as it is appointed for men to die once, and after this comes judgment."

SPIRITUAL REBIRTH AND LIFE

The Bible teaches God loves and desires to fellowship and commune with us. However, His Spirit must dwell in us through the Holy Spirit for us to fellowship and commune with Him. He has established the process through which He redeems and reconciles us to Himself. He extends His grace to and redeems us through our faith in Jesus.

Jesus indicated three actions must occur before God will redeem and reconcile us to Himself:

- We must be spiritually reborn (John 3:5-6);
- We must be converted and become like children (Matthew 18:3)); and
- We must repent of our sins (Luke 5:31-32).

God is Spirit, and we must be spiritually reborn and made spiritually alive to fellowship and commune with Him. God's Spirit must dwell in us through the Holy Spirit for Him to redeem us. We must be converted - turn away from sine - and approach God with a childlike faith for Him to reconcile us to Himself. Finally, we must repent of our sins and seek God's forgiveness through Jesus before He will allow us to come into His presence. The first action represents what God has made possible through the blood Jesus shed on a cross and the Holy Spirit. The second and third actions represents responses we must make to receive God's forgiveness and His gift of salvation through Jesus.

God's Action toward Us

Jesus indicated no one came come to God except through Him in John 14:6. Paul stated in Romans 3:23-24, 5:8-9:

> "For all have sinned and fall short of the glory of God, being justified as a gift by His grace through the redemption which is in Christ Jesus; whom God displayed publicly as a propitiation in His blood through faith. But God demonstrated His own love toward us, in that while we were yet sinners,

Christ died for us. Much more then, having now been justified by His blood, we shall be saved from the wrath of God through Him."

We have all sinned and fall short of God's glory. Jesus stood in our place "as a propitiation in His blood" for our sins whose death God publicly displayed on a cross. We are justified by Jesus' blood because His death satisfied God's death penalty for our sins. Therefore, we no longer need to fear God's wrath directed toward us because of our sins. We must approach God through the cross of Jesus (Figure 4). We are spiritually reborn through our faith in the resurrection of Jesus Christ from the dead.

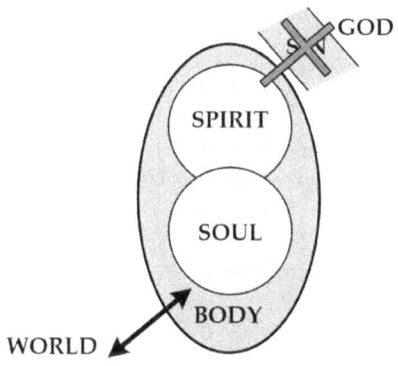

Figure 4

The Holy Spirit imparts spiritual life to us, and the blood of Jesus cleanses us of sin when we enter a reconciled relationship with God through our faith in Jesus. Jesus stated in John 6:63 the Holy Spirit gives us life. John stated in 1 John 1:7 the blood of Jesus cleanses us of sin when we walk in the Light of God. Paul stated in Titus 3:47 we are not saved by our deeds of righteousness, but we are saved by God's grace according to His mercy extended to us by the Holy Spirit through our faith in Jesus.

Paul stated in Ephesians 2:8-10:

> "For by grace you have been saved through faith; and that not of yourselves, it is the gift of God; not as a result of works, so that no one may boast. For we are His workmanship, created in Christ Jesus for good works which God prepared beforehand so that we would walk in them."

He reaffirmed we are saved by God's grace extended to us through our faith in Jesus, not by our works of righteousness. However, he added we are to perform "good works, which God prepared beforehand so that we would walk in them." We are expected to perform these good works because of the redemption we receive from God even though these works alone will not redeem and reconcile us to God. Paul further instructed us in Romans 12:2 not to be conformed to this world but to be transformed through the renewing of our minds.

Paul indicated in Romans 8:14-17 we are received by God as adopted children when we enter a relationship with Him through our faith in Jesus. We become His heirs and fellow heirs with Jesus, and we are heirs that lead to eternal life through Jesus. Therefore, Peter indicated 1 Peter 1:3-5 we have an inheritance as God's heirs that is imperishable, undefiled, will not fade away, and is reserved for us in heaven.

God has taken the initiative to establish a process through which He can redeem and reconcile us to Himself. He sent His Son, Jesus, into the world to present His word as He wanted it presented and to be a mediator of a new covenant. Jesus established and sealed this covenant by shedding His blood on a cross. This covenant fulfilled the covenant of the Law and provides the legal basis for God to redeem and reconcile us to Himself through our faith in Jesus. God has demonstrated His love for us and extended His mercy and grace to us through His Son's death. He has given us the freedom to choose how we will respond.

Our Response to God

We must do our part to receive God's gift of salvation in conjunction with Him doing His part. Jesus stated in Matthew 18:3 to enter the kingdom of God we must be converted and become like little children. The Greek word for *convert* is *strepho*, which means to twist, to turn around. The Greek word for *children* is *pardion*, which can also be translated *infants*. Jesus indicated we must turn away from our love of the world and turn toward Him to enter the kingdom of God. We must be spiritually reborn and become spiritual infants.

Peter stated in Acts 3:19:

> "Repent therefore and return, that your sins may be wiped away in order that times of refreshing may come from the presence of the Lord."

We must repent of our sins when we come to the Lord. Repentance is a heartfelt act of deep and painful regret and remorse for living a sinful life apart from God. Jesus stated in Luke 13:3 we will perish if we do not repent.

Jesus accepts us as we are with the good and bad when we repent and approach Him to seek His forgiveness. This does not mean He approves of the bad things we have done. However, He forgives us and begins the process of transforming us into the person God wants us to be through the Holy Spirit. Many are deceived into believing God will never forgive them because they have done things that are so bad. This becomes an obstacle to their receiving the redemption and reconciliation He desires to extend to them through

Jesus. God and Jesus will always forgive us when we sincerely repent of our sins and ask for Their forgiveness.

There are two specific encounters with Jesus in the New Testament that address the issue of acceptance and forgiveness. The first encounter was Jesus' encounter with a Samaritan woman at a well, described in John 4:7-42. Jesus asked the woman where her husband was during their conversation. He did this knowing she had been married five times and the man with whom she was living was not her husband. Jesus still invited her to come to Him to receive "water springing up to eternal life." He did not tell the woman to get her life in order and then come to Him. He instead invited her to come to Him as she was with the implication He would transform her life through the Holy Spirit.

The second encounter was Jesus's encounter with a woman caught in the act of adultery described in John 8:3-11. The Scribes and Pharisees brought the woman to Jesus whom they had caught in the act of committing adultery. They attempted to entrap Him by stating the Law required her to be stoned to death and asked Him what He thought they should do. Jesus stated any accuser who was without sin should cast the first stone. They all dropped their stones and left when they heard this, leaving Jesus alone with the woman. Jesus then stated to her since her accusers had not condemned her neither did He condemn her. He commanded her to go her way and sin no more. Jesus did not command the woman to go and get her life in order and then return to Him to receive His forgiveness. He forgave her while she stood before Him guilty of committing adultery.

The women in these two encounters could have been men. They could be you and me today. Jesus does not tell us to go our way, get our lives in order, and then return to Him to receive forgiveness when we approach Him for forgiveness. Instead He accepts us as we are and forgives us, knowing we are guilty of sin.

Paul instructed us in Romans 10:9-10:

> "That if you confess with your mouth, 'Jesus as Lord,' and believe in your heart that God raised him from the dead, you shall be saved; for with the heart man believes, resulting in righteousness, and with the mouth he confesses, resulting in salvation."

Paul tells you what you must do when you have not accepted Jesus into your life and been reborn or when you are not sure Jesus is present in your life. You must first repent and ask for forgiveness of your sins. You must then confess with your mouth Jesus is Lord and believe in your heart God raised Him from the dead for your sins. You must receive and accept the reality of what He has accomplished for you when He shed His blood for you on His cross.

Following is a recommended prayer for receiving salvation through Jesus:

"Father, I want to be born again. I want to have Your life-giving Spirit breathed back into my heart. I know I have done things that have been offensive to You and that have not been pleasing in Your sight. I ask You to forgive my sins and cleanse me of all unrighteousness. Jesus, I acknowledge You as Lord, the Son of God, and I believe in my heart You were raised from the dead for my sins and for me. I invite You to come into my heart and live in and through me. Take my life, Jesus, and make me the person You want me to be. Thank you, Jesus, for hearing and answering my prayer, and thank you for the knowledge that You, along with the Father and Holy Spirit, are living in and through me. Thank you for breathing spiritual life back into me and for the knowledge that I have been born again by the Spirit of God. I will serve and love You the rest of my life."

The Holy Spirit washes us with the blood of Jesus and cleanses us of our sins when we repent (turn away from our old rebellious way of living) and accept what God has accomplished for us through Jesus on a cross, (1 Corinthians 6:11, Titus 3:5). We are reborn, and God's Spirit through the Holy Spirit takes up residence in and nurtures us. Paul stated in Romans 8:14-17:

"For all who are being led by the Spirit of God, these are sons of God. For you have not received a spirit of slavery leading to fear again, but you have received a spirit of adoption as sons by which we cry out, 'Abba! Father!' The Spirit Himself bears witness with our spirit that we are children of God, and if children, heirs also, heirs of God and fellow heirs with Christ, if indeed we suffer with Him in order that we may also be glorified with Him."

We become children of God when we receive and accept the redemption and reconciliation God extends to us through our faith in Jesus. The Holy Spirit regenerates our spirit and begins the process of renewing our mind and transforming our heart. Paul indicated when these occur in our life:

- We become new creatures when Jesus lives in us (2 Corinthians 5:17); and
- We will be strengthened with power through faith, be able to comprehend and know the love of Jesus that surpasses knowledge, and be filled to the fullness of God (Ephesians 3:14-19).

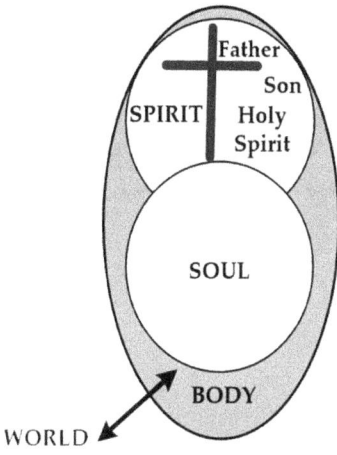

Figure 5

God (Father, Son and Holy Spirit) resides in us when we are spiritually reborn (Figure 5). Paul stated in 1 Corinthians 3:16:

> "Do you not know that you are a temple of God and that the Spirit of God dwells in you?"

We become a temple of God and a new creation in Jesus when we are spiritually reborn. Our spirit and soul are energized and nurtured by the Holy Spirit. Paul stated in Galatians 2:20:

> "I have been crucified with Christ; and it is no longer I who live, but Christ lives in me; and the life which I now live in the flesh I live by faith in the Son of God, who loved me and gave Himself up for me."

God through the Holy Spirit calls us and enables us to respond to His call. God, Jesus and the Holy Spirit dwell in us after we come to God through our faith in Jesus. The Holy Spirit equips us to trust and obey God and Jesus in our relationship with Them. God reveals Himself to us through His word in the Bible and the presence of the Holy Spirit in our life. The Holy Spirit initiates and continues the process of transforming our heart through the renewing of our mind so we can discern God's will in our life (Romans 12:2) as we spiritually grow and mature.

CHAPTER 5
STRUCTURE OF OUR SOUL AND SPIRIT

OUR SOUL

Paul stated in 1 Thessalonians 5:23:

> "Now may the God of peace Himself sanctify you entirely; and may your spirit and soul and body be preserved complete, without blame at the coming of our Lord Jesus Christ."

Our soul is an immaterial formless entity that is separable from our body that:\

- Possesses memory
- Acquires knowledge
- Experiences emotions
- Creates thoughts
- Forms habits
- Initiates actions

Our soul, which is comprised of our mind and heart, instinctively moves us toward God. David stated in Psalm 139:13-16:

> "For You formed my inward parts;
> You wove me in my mother's womb.
> I will give thanks to You, for I am fearfully and wonderfully made;
> Wonderful are Your works,
> And my soul knows it very well.
> My frame was not hidden from You,
> When I was made in secret,
> And skillfully wrought in the depths of the earth;
> Your eyes have seen my unformed substance;
> And in Your book were written
> The days that were ordained for me,
> When as yet there was not one of them."

David implied in this Psalm our soul motivates us to be the person God has uniquely created us to be. It is our moral compass that leads and enables us to live life with dignity, integrity and humility when it is nurtured by God through the presence of the Holy Spirit.

THE STRUCTURE OF AND PROCESSES WITHIN OUR SOUL

Chapter 4 indicates our soul is the structure of our mind and heart - of memory, intellect, personality and character (Figure 2). Our soul governs how our spirit encounters, interprets and responds to life experiences through our body according to the way it assimilates and processes information it receives and experiences it encounters.

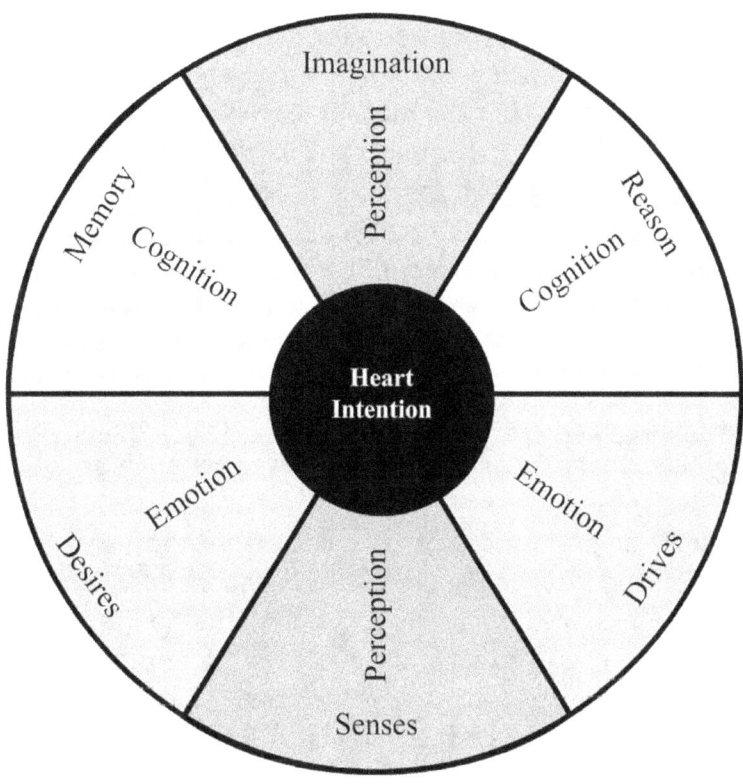

Figure 6

Chris Webb in his book, *The Fire of the Word: Meeting God on Holy Ground* (2011), presented the pictorial representation of our soul shown in Figure 6. The figure indicates our soul supports six actions and four processes. The six actions are: senses, imagination, memory, reason, desires and drives. The four processes are: perception, cognition, emotion and intention. Webb indicated the visual representation of the soul in Figure 6 was derived from ancient writings by Plato, Aristotle and the apostle Paul.

Inputs to our soul enter through the actions of *senses* and *imagination* in our mind. *Senses* receive information through our five physical senses (sight, hearing, touch, taste and smell) from the physical world and through our spirit from the spiritual realm.

Imagination supplies supplemental information that further develops and embellishes information received into our mind. *Senses* and *imagination* allow us to receive information from God in the spiritual realm and from family, work and other environments where we are active in the physical world around us. *Senses* and *imagination* initiate the process of *perception*. *Perception* is the process through which we develop a coherent and unified awareness of the information we receive into our mind.

The actions of *memory* and *reason* interact in our mind to initiate the process of *cognition*. *Memory* is our repository of stored information received into our mind by *senses* and *imagination*. *Reason* is the action of our mind in which we assimilate and process this information in an orderly and systematic manner. *Cognition* is the process in our mind by which we acquire knowledge and gain insights and wisdom from this information. *Reason* and *cognition* combine to form *intellect*. The process of *cognition* facilitates the development of life skills. These skills enable us to engage in our life activities and challenges.

Desires and *drives* are actions within our heart. *Desires* are yearnings that predispose us to want to do certain activities and engage in specific tasks. *Drives* are strong urges that motivate and move us to do the activities and complete the tasks. *Desires* and *drives* initiate the process of *emotion* in our heart. *Emotion* is derived from the Latin words *emovere*, which means to disturb, and *movere*, which means to move. *Emotion* as it is used here is the process in our heart that motivates and moves us to act on information we process in our mind.

Our heart assimilates and processes outcomes from the processes of *perception*, *cognition* and *emotion* and initiates the process of *intention*. *Intention* is derived from the Latin word *intendere*, which means stretch, turn one's attention to. *Intention* as it is used here is the process that directs us to act in specific ways. It for example directs us to initiate a deliberate course of action, to form a new life habit, or to enter a new relationship. *Intention* is the process in our heart that directs us to stretch forth to engage in life's activities and challenges.

Figure 7 presents a more descriptive illustration of the actions and processes that occur within our soul. The development of this figure came to me in a dream. The emotional, psychological and functional interrelations between the actions and processes are complex. However, Figure 7 can be used with the preceding discussion to develop a more complete understanding of the interrelationships between the actions and processes shown in Figure 6.

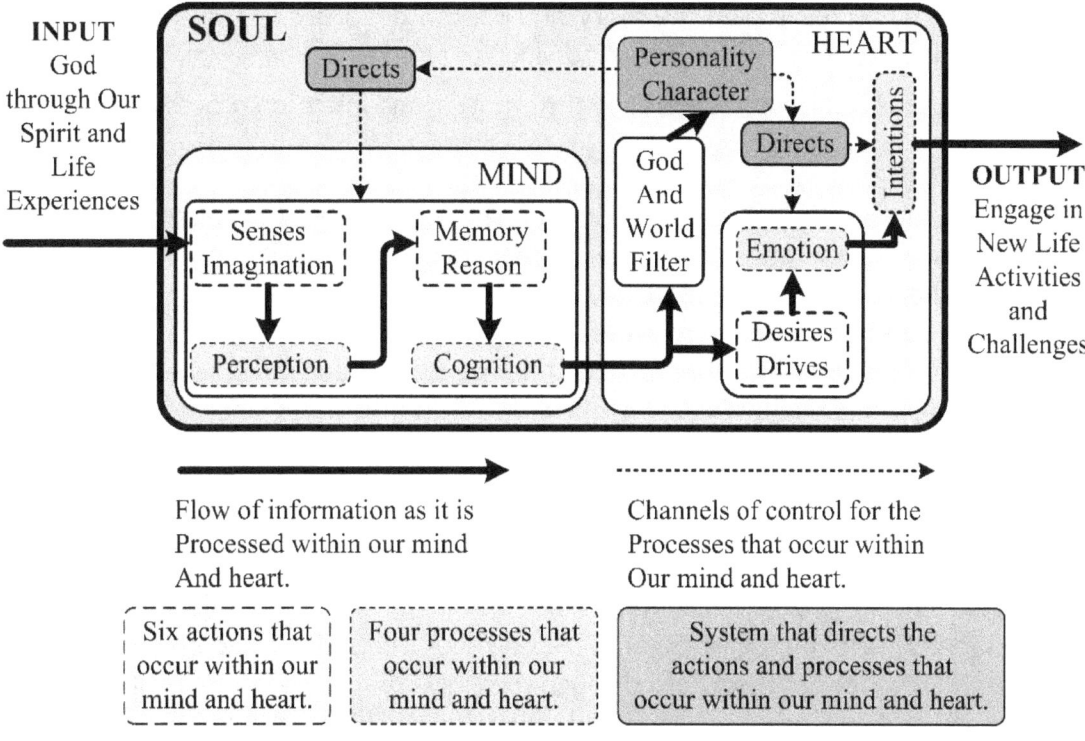

Figure 7

Figure 7 identifies additional processes that occur within and between our mind and heart. A *God and World Filter* is located between the symbol for the cognition process and the symbol for our personality and character. This filter can be referred to as the *God Site* in our soul. It performs an important function in the development of our personality and character. Its filter characteristics develop as we emotionally, psychologically and spiritually grow and mature. The development of the characteristics of this filter is influenced by two primary sources: God and the world. The filter characteristics most often are defined by God's laws and spiritual life principles when we live and grow up in an environment that affirms the existence of God and His presence in our life. The filter characteristics most often are defined by world and cultural norms and customs that may be hostile toward God when we live and grow up in an environment that denies His existence and may be hostile toward Him. The filter characteristics in many cases contain elements that are defined by both God and the world. This often results in struggles and conflicts within our soul that will be discussed later in this chapter.

Figure 7 indicates our personality and character direct:

- The senses, imagination, memory and reason actions and the perception and cognition processes within our mind, and
- The desires and drives actions and the emotion and intention processes within our heart.

Outputs from the cognition process in our mind with their associated knowledge, insights and wisdom continually influence the development of our personality and character as we assimilate and process life experiences. These outputs are filtered and often modified by the *God and World Filter* before they affect the development of or initiate changes in our personality and character. The effects of this filtering process depend on whether the filter characteristics are defined by God or by the world. This influences whether we grow into a life and life activities that honor and are obedient to God or into a life and life activities that reject and may be hostile toward God.

The redemption and reconciliation we receive from God through Jesus are gifts. God (Father, Son and Holy Spirit) takes up residence in us when we enter a relationship with Him through Jesus. How this occurs is a mystery, but it occurs. The place of this residence is the *God and World Filter* in our heart (Figure 7). It becomes the *God Site* in our soul when God is present. He reaches out from here through the Holy Spirit to begin the healing process of hurting and broken areas in our spirit and soul (mind and heart) and to initiate processes that will facilitate the transformation of our personality and character necessary for us to become obedient to Him and Jesus.

God requires us to read, study and internalize His word in the Bible to grow and mature in our relationship with Him through Jesus and the Holy Spirit. He reveals Himself to us through the Holy Spirit as we enter and continue this process, and He continues His healing process within our spirit and soul. God's, Jesus' and the Holy Spirit's imprint on our mind becomes clearer and more focused, and Their presence in our heart becomes stronger and more active as we grow and mature in our relationship with them.

The Holy Spirit adapts our personality and character to be sensitive, responsive and obedient to God's and Jesus' presence in our life as we grow in our understanding of and continue to internalize God's word in the Bible. This focuses Their presence on the perception and cognition processes that renew our mind and inserts Their presence into the emotion and intention processes that transform our heart. Paul stated relative to these processes in Philippians 4:6-7:

> "Be anxious for nothing, but in everything by prayer and supplication with thanksgiving let your request be made known to God. And the peace of God, which surpasses all comprehension, will guard your hearts and your minds in Christ Jesus."

Paul continued regarding our relationship with God in Philippians 4:8-9:

> "Finally, brethren, whatever is true, whatever is honorable, whatever is right, whatever is pure, whatever is lovely, whatever is of good repute, if there is any excellence and if anything worthy of praise, dwell on these things. The things you have learned and received and heard and seen in me, practice these things, and the God of peace will be with you."

God through the Holy Spirit transforms the characteristics of the *God and World Filter* in our heart. This filter becomes the *God Site* in our heart when we initially grow up or live in an environment that rejects and is hostile toward God, and we later enter a reconciled relationship with Him through Jesus. The renewing and transforming processes described above will begin when this occurs. These processes can begin at any age or stage in our life.

OUR SOUL WHEN NURTURED BY GOD

Our soul is the seat of our conscience, insight and sensitivity. God designed our mind to be the repository of His spiritual knowledge, insights and wisdom. A God consciousness develops in the God Site in our heart that facilitates the transformation of our personality and character as we fellowship and grow in our relationship with God through Jesus. This is essential for Him to renew our mind and transform our heart. The Holy Spirit then opens our mind and heart to receive, understand and assimilate God's spiritual laws and principles that govern our life. We grow in our understanding of the kind of person God has created us to be and how He wants us to interact with and relate to Him, others and the world around us as we read, study and internalize His word in the Bible and enter into fellowship with other Christians. We learn our life is governed by these moral and spiritual laws and spiritual life principles, and the Holy Spirit creates within us the desire and gives us the ability to live according to them.

Our soul is also the seat of our creativity, inspiration and motivation. Our mind and heart process and assimilate information they receive from the spiritual realm of God and the physical world where we live, and they direct how we respond to this information. Life and meaning are given to ideas and beliefs that develop within our mind, and our heart inspires and motivates us to achieve tasks and to act on convictions that evolve from them.

Individuals whose minds and hearts are nurtured by the Holy Spirit:

- Experience the love, mercy, grace and forgiveness God gives to them through His Son, Jesus;

- Become sensitive to and reach out to and love others in the same way He reaches out to and loves them through Jesus.
- Are always able to approach life with a positive and balanced perspective;
- Have the energy, resiliency and motivation necessary to endure hardships and overcome obstacles they encounter;
- Develop insights into life and their relationship with God and others that are clearly inspired and motivated by the Holy Spirit;
- Radiate an enthusiasm for life that is contagious; and
- Have a zest for life that inspires and motivates others.

YEARNINGS WITHIN OUR SOUL

Our soul is created with built-in yearnings of the heart that drive us to move beyond ourself to seek meaning in life and our own distinct reality and destiny. Richard D. Grant and Andrea Wells Miller in their book, *Recovering Connections* (1993) and J. Keith Miller in his book, *The Secret Life of the Soul* (1997), indicate there are four basic yearnings within our soul. They are the yearning for:

- Perfect parenting,
- Perfect companionship,
- Perfect power and freedom, and
- Perfect meaning.

These yearnings begin at birth with our initial relationship with our parents. They progress to relationships with others, ultimately resulting in a relationship with God. They begin with our being dependent on our parents for meeting our physical, emotional and spiritual needs. We progress to where we want to be free and in control of our life, being dependent only on ourself for meeting these needs. We ultimately become dependent on God through the Holy Spirit for meeting these needs as we develop a relationship with Him through Jesus. Yearnings within our soul that occur in infancy are characterized by our being selfish, self-centered and caring only about satisfying our own physical, emotional and spiritual needs. We discover as we grow to adulthood true meaning in life is only achieved when we yield our life in obedience to God through Jesus and reach beyond ourself in selfless love to meet the legitimate needs of others.

Miller (The Secret Life of the Soul, 1997) indicated the above four yearnings can only be truly satisfied by God as Father, Son and Holy Spirit:

- Our yearning for a perfect parent is only satisfied when we enter an obedient and trusting relationship with God as Father.

- Our yearning for perfect companionship is only satisfied when we enter a surrendered relationship with Jesus within the fellowship and support of a local Christian community.

- Our yearning for perfect power and freedom is only satisfied when we invite the Holy Spirit into our life and allow Him to renew our mind and transform our heart.

- Our yearning for perfect meaning is only satisfied when our mind is renewed, our heart is transformed, and we seek and do God's will for our life.

Our personality develops the positive attributes God desires us to have and our moral and ethical values associated with our character become Christlike when our soul is nurtured by the Holy Spirit.

OUR SPIRIT WHEN NURTURED BY GOD

We will examine the functions of our spirit when we are spiritually alive, and our soul and spirit are nourished and nurtured by the Holy Spirit. Some functions are supported by the Bible while others are based on life experiences and observations (John and Paula Sandford, *Healing the Wounded Spirit*, 1985).

The first and most important function of our spirit is to worship God. Worship is our response to God's grace and His gift of redemption and reconciliation through our faith in Jesus. Paul stated in Romans 12:1:

> "Therefore I urge you therefore, brethren, by the mercies of God, to present your bodies a living and holy sacrifice, acceptable to God, which is your spiritual service and worship."

God has created us for His good pleasure to love and serve Him. Jesus stated in Mark 12:30 we are to love God with all our heart, mind, soul and strength. We are to focus our attention on, direct our affection toward, and use our talents for Him in everything we do. Jesus stated in John 4:23-24 we must worship God in spirit and truth. Real worship is a lifestyle through which we affirm the love we have for God. Everything we say and do in life must affirm His presence in our life and be done in a manner that brings Him glory and honor.

We approach God through corporate and private worship. Corporate worship is where we participate in singing and lifting praises, adoration and thanksgiving to God in fellowship with other Christians. Psalm 100:1-5 states:

"Shout joyfully to the LORD, all the earth. Serve the LORD with gladness; come before Him with joyful singing. Know that the LORD Himself is God; it is He who has made us and not we ourselves; we are His people and the sheep of His pasture. Enter His gates with thanksgiving and His courts with praise. Give thanks to Him; bless His name. For the LORD is good; His loving kindness is everlasting and His faithfulness to all generations."

Corporate worship and fellowship are where we recognize God has created us and has facilitated our receiving all we possess. They are where we experience His love for use and receive strength to persevere.

Private worship and devotions are where we spend focused personal times with God. Our devotions are times when we approach Him through prayer and study His word in the Bible. We communicate with God through prayer, and He communicates with us through His word given to us in the Bible.

We receive knowledge of God's spiritual life principles that govern our life as we study His word in the Bible when we are spiritually alive. The Holy Spirit gives meaning and life to these principles and imprints them onto our mind and subconscious mind as we study and internalize them. We grow in our wisdom and insights related to these principles as we enter a deeper and more personal relationship with God through the guidance of the Holy Spirit. This enables us to incorporate these principles into our life more effectively.

God speaks to our mind and subconscious mind through the Holy Spirit, and we know He hears us when we speak to Him through prayer and lift our praises and adoration to Him in worship. Our soul is energized and receives strength from God through the Holy Spirit when we are spiritually alive. This enable us to engage life's challenges, endure its hardships and live a life that glorifies God and is built on the foundation of His spiritual life principles and laws.

Our spirit plays an important role in our interaction and communication with other persons. Our spirit reaches out through time and space to interact with others. We sense their presence, emotions and sensitivity with our spirit. Sometimes without any verbal communication our spirit senses an individual's acceptance or rejection. Our spirit empathizes with and tunes into another person's feelings and emotions. We often desire to interact with and develop a relationship with a person when our spirit resonates with that person's spirit. We avoid a person when our spirit is repulsed. We have a sensitivity toward others that lowers barriers and establishes channels of communication with them necessary to develop and grow lasting relationships when we are spiritually alive.

Our spirit gives us stamina and buoyancy to confront life's challenges and hardships. We have the stamina and buoyancy to confront life's challenges and hardships and persevere when we are spiritually alive. Proverbs 18:14 states, "The spirit of a man can endure his sickness, but a broken spirit who can bear?" We can persevere through challenging and difficult times when our spirit is nourished and strengthened by the Holy Spirit. We can work through and look beyond these times with eyes of faith to see and experience God working in our life to bring us into a closer and more intimate relationship with Him.

Our spirit becomes united with the spirit of our spouse in marriage. We become one flesh with our spouse in marriage. God stated in Genesis 2:24:

> "For this cause a man shall leave his father and his mother and shall cleave to his wife; and they shall become one flesh."

Jesus reaffirmed this in Mark 10:6-8 where he stated:

> "But from the beginning of creation, God made them male and female. For this cause a man shall leave his father and mother and the two shall become one flesh; consequently they are no longer two, but one flesh."

The Bible implies marriage is consummated in the sexual union between a husband and wife. Paul implied this in 1 Corinthians 6:16-18:

> "Or do you not know that the one who joins himself to a harlot is one body with her? For [Jesus] says, 'The two will become one flesh." But the one who joins himself to the Lord is one spirit with Him. Flee immorality. Every other sin that a man commits is outside the body, but the immoral man sins against his own body.'"

God has created marriage to be a holy and sacred covenant relationship between a husband and wife. It is the most intimate and sacred of all human covenants. Marriage is a relationship where all the functions of our spirit are active.

The spirits of a husband and wife resonant with each other when their spirits are alive and nourished by the Holy Spirit. Weaknesses and shortcomings of one are accepted and buoyed up by the strengths of the other. A husband and wife nurture and help each other, and they work to meet and satisfy each other's needs. They find their completeness in each other, and the most holy and sacred form of this completeness is manifested as they unselfishly give themselves to each other in sexual union. A husband and wife affirm each other's right to develop unique identities within the context of their marriage relationship as they experience life together. However, they develop these identities in the context of becoming one in spirit and developing a unified identity in their marriage that is formed through shared experiences.

STRUGGLES WITHIN OUR SOUL

God creates and brings each one of us into this world for specific purposes, and He has established behavioral boundaries. He gives us the freedom to choose if we will live according to the purposes for which He has created us and within the behavioral boundaries He has established. Our mind and heart will develop under the guidance of and be nurtured by the Holy Spirit when we choose to live according to God's will through Jesus. Our soul will be in communication with God through our spirit. However, this does not always occur in our life.

The Bible indicates our soul is a battleground in our life between good and evil, righteousness and unrighteousness, and obedience and disobedience. Our soul is where we decide we will live a life of dignity, integrity and humility in obedience to God through Jesus or a life of disobedience to God where we seek those things the world says we are entitled. How we resolve the struggles within our soul determines whether our life will be controlled by:

- The presence and guidance of God through the Holy Spirit, or
- Our desire to be in control and seek those things the world says are important.

The choices we make will affect our ability to find true meaning and purpose in life and to develop a healthy sense of self-esteem and self-worth.

The development and growth of our soul is influenced by our needs to:

- Be nurtured and supported (perfect parenting);
- Seek and enter into relationships with others (perfect companionship);
- Achieve success and status in life (perfect power and freedom); and
- Find purpose in life and develop self-esteem and self-worth (perfect meaning).

The development and growth of our soul occurs in a fallen world that has been corrupted by sin and where we struggle with our sin nature. Our sin nature predisposes us to be hostile toward God and to seek what the world says is true and important.

We seek to satisfy the four yearnings of our soul in a hostile environment. In this environment:

- We sometimes do not have perfect parents as a child. Our parents may not give us the affection, support and nurturing we need. There are those who are emotionally, physically and sexually abused as children by their parents or other adults.

- We do not enter perfect relationships. We enter relationships where we are teased, tormented, rejected, used, manipulated, abused, molested, and assaulted. We enter personal, business and marriage relationships that fail.

- We do not make wise decisions in our quest for success and status in life. We make decisions that compromise our character and integrity. Just as we may become victims of others in their pursuit for success and status, we may make decisions and institute actions that victimize others. We experience disappointment and failure in our quest for success and status.

- Problems and failures we experience in our attempts to satisfy the first three yearnings of our soul can cause us to lose purpose and meaning in our life and leave us with a sense of a lack of self-esteem and self-worth. Our life can be devastated by negative experiences and appear to be out-of-control.

Consequences associated with not positively addressing our failures to satisfy the yearnings of our soul result in wounds within our soul and spirit. These wounds can derail God's purpose for our life and His desired development of our personality and character.

We become angry at and shut God out of our life when we experience serious wounds within our soul and spirit. This separates us from Him, and the continued development of our personality and character occurs in a manner that shields us from being wounded again. This intensifies battles, struggles and conflicts that occur within our soul.

Thoughts and what some describe as voices occur within our mind when our soul processes the battles, struggles and conflicts that occur within it. These thoughts/voices come from three sources:

- **The spiritual realm of God through angels and the Holy Spirit.** Thoughts/voices that originate from the spiritual realm of God direct us toward God who desires to heal our emotional and spiritual wounds. They affirm our value, dignity and worth in the eyes of God, and they encourage us to seek a life that is acceptable and pleasing to Him. They lead us to accept and receive the love, mercy, grace and forgiveness God extends to us through Jesus. They encourage us to give the Holy Spirit permission to enter our life to heal our emotional and spiritual wounds and to begin or continue the processes of renewing our mind and transforming our heart.

- **The spiritual realm of Satan through demonic sources.** Thoughts/voices that originate from the spiritual realm of Satan accuse and condemn us and work to draw us away from and make us hostile toward God. They attempt to shame us and take away our sense of value, dignity and worth. They create within us a sense that we are stupid, careless, worthless, etc. They imply we deserve the failures and bad and devastating experiences that have occurred in our life. They seek to drive us into a state of hopelessness and despair.

- **Our own mind.** Thoughts/voices that originate in our mind and subconscious mind represent our perception of the state of our life. They reflect our concerns, fears, dreams, desires, plans, etc. They also reflect our emotional response to the thoughts/voices that come from the spiritual realms of God and Satan. How we process these thoughts/voices will either enhance our sense of self-worth and dignity or draw us into a deeper sense of hopelessness and despair.

The affirming thoughts/voices in our mind from the spiritual realm of God are ignored or repressed when our personality and character develop independent of God. The shaming and condemning thoughts/voices from the spiritual realm of Satan then become dominant, and the thoughts/voice originating within our own mind often condemn and shame us.

Thoughts/voices originating in our mind that condemn and shame us can occur whether we have entered a relationship with God through Jesus. This is certain to occur when we reject Jesus' claim on our life and are separated from God. However, it can occur when we invite Jesus into our life but do not give the Holy Spirit permission to perform His renewing and transforming processes. The Holy Spirit will not begin these processes in our soul until we give Him permission. The nurturing presence of God in our life is impaired when we fail to give the Holy Spirit permission to function within our soul.

Miller (*The Secret Life of the Soul*, 1997) indicated we enter activities directed at quieting and escaping the shaming and condemning thoughts/voices that exist in our mind when our personality and character develop independent of God. This leads us into compulsive and addictive behaviors. We may become overachievers and workaholics, hoping to find purpose and meaning in life and escape these thoughts/voices. We may become addicted to alcohol, drugs, pornography and sex because of their nagging presence. We ultimately discover these behaviors do not afford us any relief or escape. We experience a greater sense of hopelessness and despair as we enter further into these behaviors.

There are several potential negative consequences on our life when we allow our personality and character to develop independent of God.

- Spiritual communication with God is seriously impaired or cut off. As a result, our soul is unable to receive spiritual information from and to be nurtured by the Holy Spirit. Paul stated in 1 Corinthians 2:14:

"But a nature man does not accept the things of the Spirit of God; for they are foolishness to him and he cannot understand them, because they are spiritually appraised."

- We become controlled by our interaction with the world when we take control of our life away from God, Jesus and the Holy Spirit. We become self-reliant and hostile toward God instead of developing a dependent, nurturing and loving relationship with Him.

- We are blind to God's absolute moral and spiritual laws that govern our life. The safeguards He has given us to keep our life in harmony with Him, others, ourself and the world are inoperable; they are dormant. Consequently, our life becomes controlled by our physical desires and appetites and by what the world says is important rather than by what God says is important. This increases our independence from and hostility toward God.

- We tend to become manipulative and controlling in nature and to relate to others in a way that can cause them to be apprehensive and defensive. We are unable to be compassionate and sensitive to others because we are unable to experience God's love and compassion. This results in the erection of barriers that impede the development of meaningful and trusting relationships.

- We are overcome and discouraged by hardships and crises in our life. We lack the stamina and buoyancy necessary to effectively confront them in a positive manner. They become devastating and destructive, particularly when we cannot see through or beyond them to the better times that will lie ahead. At a minimum, they become events that result in the development of a negative and defeated attitude. In more serious situations, they result in serious emotional and spiritual problems.

The beautiful story that runs throughout the Bible is God is loving, caring and patient. He continually reaches out to us with an invitation to come to Him through Jesus. God will remain in the background as long as we want to be in control of our life and allow our personality and character to develop independent of Him. He will permit us to sink deeper into hopelessness and despair until we ultimately give up and surrender to and seek Him. The voice of the Holy Spirit will quietly and gently break through the shaming and condemning thoughts/voices in our mind at this point to affirm God loves, forgives and desires to enter a loving, healing and nurturing relationship with us though His Son, Jesus.

We can begin to approach God on a more intimate bases through a process known as *Lectio Divina*. This process that is traditionally used in Catholicism to read and study the Bible can be used by anyone. It has four steps:

Read God's word in the Bible with reverance and the inspiration of the Holy Spirit.

Meditate by focusing our thoughts on what we have read.

Pray over the relevance of what we have read to our life.

Contemplate on how we plan to apply what we have read to our life.

When we surrender and yield ourself to God through our faith and trust in and obedience to Jesus:

- The Holy Spirit will:
  1. Enter our life and initiate processes that result in the healing of our soul and spirit, the renewal of our mind, and the transformation of our heart, and
  2. Facilitate the growth of the positive personality attributes and Christlike character God has created within us.
- The dominant thoughts/voices in our mind will be those from the spiritual realm of God. They will:
  1. Affirm our value, dignity and worth in the eyes of God;
  2. Affirm our relationship with God through our faith in Jesus;
  3. Encourage us to live a life that is built on the foundation of God's spiritual life principle revealed to us in the Bible; and
  4. Transform the thoughts/voices that originate in our mind and subconscious mind to be compatible with the thoughts/voices we receive from the spiritual realm of God.
- We will develop and grow in our ability to live a life of faith and trust in and obedience to God through our faith and trust in and obedience to Jesus.
- Our soul will commune with and be nurtured and strengthen by God through actions of the Holy Spirit in our life.
- We will find true meaning and purpose in and for our life and experience true freedom and joy.

CHAPTER 6
JESUS - GOD'S SON AND OUR SAVIOR AND LORD OF OUR LIFE

JESUS AND THE BIBLE

God's love and plan for the redemption of His creation through Jesus after the fall of Adam and Eve in the Garden of Eden are the central themes throughout the Bible. Events prophesied about Jesus's life in the Old Testament were fulfilled by Him during His life in the New Testament. Table 2 lists some of the major events in Jesus' life that were prophesied in the Old Testament that were fulfilled by Him in the New Testament. According to Peter Stoner in his book, *Science Speaks: An Evaluation of Certain Christian Evidences* (1963), the probability the nine prophesies in the table that are preceded by an * were fulfilled by Jesus during His lifetime is 1 in 10^{17} (1 followed by 17 zeroes). 10^{17} silver dollars will cover the whole state of Texas to a depth of two feet. Imagine the probability of being able to pluck out one silver dollar that has been marked and randomly placed in that many silver dollars.

Table 2

Events in Life	Old Testament Prophesies	Fulfilled in the New Testament
Born of a virgin	Isaiah 7:14	Matthew 1:23,25
*Born in Bethlehem	Micah 5.2	Matthew 2:1 Luke 2:4-7
Herod to massacre infants	Jeremiah 31:15	Matthew 2:16
Would heal people	Isaiah 53:4	Matthew 8:16-17
*To be preceded by	Isaiah 40:3	Matthew 3:1-2
a messenger	Malachi 3:1	John 1:23, Mark 7:33-35
Would teach in parables	Isaiah 6:9-10	Matthew 13:10-15
Would be rejected	Psalm 69:8	John 1:11, 7:5
		Isaiah 53:3
*To enter Jerusalem on a donkey	Zechariah 9:9	Mathew 21:4-5

*To be betrayed by a friend	Psalm 41:9, 55:12-14	Matthew 10:4, 26:49-50
		John 13:21
*To be betrayed for 30 pieces of silver	Psalm 41:9, Zechariah 11:12-13	Matthew 26:14-16, 21- 25
*Silver to be used to buy Potter's field	Zechariah 11:13	Matthew 27:7
To be forsaken by His disciples	Zechariah 13:7	Matthew 26:31
		Mark 14:27,50
*To be dumb before accusers	Isaiah 53:7	Matthew 27:12-19
To be wounded and bruised	Isaiah 53:5 Zachariah 13:6	Matthew 27:26
*Hands and feet to be pierced	Psalm 22:16 Zechariah 12:10	Luke 23:33 John 20:25
*To be crucified between two thieves	Isaiah 53:12	Matthew 27:38 Mark15:27-28 Luke 22:37
Would rise from the dead	Psalm 16:10	Matthew 28:2-7
Would ascend into heaven	Psalm 24:7-10	Mark 16:19 Luke 24:51

JESUS - GOD'S AGENT FOR REDEMPTION AND RECONCILIATION

God set into motion how He planned to redeem fallen humanity following the fall of Adam and Eve in the Garden of Eden (Genesis 3). He accomplished this by impregnating a virgin named Mary through an act of the Holy Spirit so His Son, Jesus, could be born into the world. John stated in John 1:1-2:

> "In the beginning was the Word, and the Word was with God, and the Word was God. He was in the beginning with God."

Jesus is the Word who was with God in the beginning. Paul reaffirmed this in Colossians 1:15-17, 21-23 where he stated:

> "And He is the image of the invisible God, the firstborn of all creation. For in Him all things were created, both in the heavens and on earth, visible and invisible, whether thrones or dominions or rulers or authorities - all things have been created through Him and for Him. And He is before all things, and in Him all things hold together. ... And although you were formerly alienated

and hostile in mind, engaged in evil deeds, yet He has now reconciled you in His fleshly body through death, in order to present you before Him holy and blameless and beyond reproach - if indeed you continue in the faith firmly established and steadfast, and not moved away from the hope of the gospel that you have heard, which was proclaimed in all creation under heaven, and of which I, Paul, was made a minister."

Jesus is "the image of the invisible God," and all things in heaven and on earth have been created by and for Him. John stated in John 1:3 all things have come into being by Jesus. He is "the firstborn of all creation," and all things in creation are held together in and by Him.

The Bible refers to Jesus in many ways. It refers to Him as:

- God (Hebrews 1:8-9),
- The Son of God (Matthew 16:16),
- The Word (John 1:1),
- The King of kings and Lord of lords (1 Timothy 6:15),
- Our Messiah (John 1:41), and
- Our Savior (1 John 4:14).

These refer to Jesus' deity. Jesus is also referred to as:

- The Son of Man (Luke 9:22),
- The Son of David (Matthew 9:27), and
- Man (John 10:5).

These refer to His humanity. Jesus referred to Himself as:

- The good shepherd (John 1:14, 27),
- The bread of life (John 6:35),
- The light of the world (John 8:12),
- The door (John 10:9),
- The resurrection and life (John 11:25-26),
- The way, the truth and the life (John 14:6), and
- The true vine (John 15:1-2).

These point to the facts Jesus:

- Reestablished the kingdom of God on earth and in the hearts of men and women;
- Is the king of God's Kingdom;
- Is the door through which we must pass to enter the kingdom of God; and
- Is the true vine through which the Spirit of God passes to breathe spiritual life into the hearts of men and women and to empower them to live according to the spiritual and life principles and laws of God.

Jesus stated in John 14:6, "no one comes to the Father but through Me."

JESUS - HE CAME TO ESTABLISH A NEW COVENANT IN HIS BLOOD AND SEND THE HOLY SPIRIT

Jesus came into this world from the presence of God. He stated in John 6:38:

> "For I have come down from heaven, not to do My own will, but the will of Him who sent Me."

He also stated in John 4:34, "My food is to do the will of Him who sent me, and to accomplish His work." Jesus came to reestablish the kingdom of God in the world. The disobedience of Adam introduced sin and death into God's creation and separated us from God. The perfect obedience of Jesus provides the way we can be reconciled to God and receive eternal life. Paul stated in Romans 5:18-21:

> "So then, as through one transgression there resulted condemnation to all men, even so through one act of righteousness there resulted justification of life to all men. For as through the one man's disobedience the many were made sinners, even so through the obedience of the One the many will be made righteous. The Law came in so that the transgressions would increase; but where sin increases, grace abounded all the more, so that, as sin reigned in death, even so grace would reign through righteousness to eternal life through Jesus Christ our Lord."

Jesus came to reveal the nature and character of God and His kingdom as God wanted them revealed in His own person. He came to bear witness to the truth of God that gives us freedom and life. He stated in John 8:31, 51:

"If you continue in My word, then you are truly disciples of Mine; and you will know the truth, and the truth will make you free. ... Truly, truly, I say to you, if anyone keeps My word he will never see death."

Jesus came to fulfill the Law. He stated in Matthew 5:17:

"Do not think that I came to abolish the Law or the Prophets; I did not come to abolish but to fulfill."

God gave us the Law to expose our sinful nature. The Law can only expose and convict us of sin; it cannot redeem or save us from the eternal consequences of sin. It is impossible to obey the 613 commandments of the Law. Therefore, it has become a curse to us that results in death. We cannot free ourself from this curse.

Jesus fulfilled the Law by establishing a new covenant that superseded the covenant of the Law. He sealed this new covenant with His blood shed on a cross. Jesus stated in Luke 22:20, "This cup which is poured out for you is the new covenant in My blood." In Hebrews 7:22, the author stated, "So much the more also Jesus has become the guarantee of a better covenant." The covenant Jesus established through His blood redeems and frees us from: the curse of the Law and reconciles us to God. Paul stated regarding this in Galatians 3:10-14:

"For as many as are of the works of the Law are under a curse, for it is written, 'Curst is everyone who does not abide by all things written in the book of the Law, to perform them.' (Deuteronomy 27:26) Now that no one is justified by the Law before God is evident; for 'The righteous man shall live by faith.' However, the Law is not of faith; on the contrary, 'He who practices them shall live by them.' (Leviticus 18:5) Christ redeemed us from the curse of the Law, having become a curse for us - for it is written, 'Cursed is everyone who hangs on a tree.' (Deuteronomy 21:22-23) - in order that in Christ Jesus the blessing of Abraham might come to the Gentiles, so that we would receive the promise of the Spirit through faith."

Jesus is the mediator of the new covenant He established and sealed with His blood. In Hebrews 9:15-16, the author wrote:

"And for this reason [Jesus] is the mediator of a new covenant, in order that since a death has taken place for the redemption of the transgressions that were committed under the first covenant, those who have been called may receive the promise of the eternal inheritance. For where a covenant is, there must of necessity be the death of the one who made it."

This new covenant is an eternal covenant, and it is the legal means through which our redemption and reconciliation to God can occur. This covenant allows us to approach God through Jesus to receive His grace, mercy and love. In Hebrews 10:15-18, the author stated the Holy Spirit said with respect to this covenant:

> "'This is the covenant that I will make with them after those days', says the LORD; 'I will put My Laws upon their hearts, and on their minds I will write them.' (Jeremiah 31:33) He then says, 'And their sins and their lawless deeds I will remember no more.' (Jeremiah 31:34) Now where there is forgiveness of these things, there is no longer any offering for sin."

This new covenant established through Jesus enables those who trust in and are obedient to Jesus to receive the eternal inheritance, and God will no longer remember "their sins and their lawless deeds."

Jesus came to be our savior. John stated in 1 John 4:14:

> "We have seen and testify that the Father has sent the Son to be the Savior of the world."

In Hebrews 2:9, the author stated:

> "But we do see Him who has been made for a little while lower than angels, namely, Jesus, because of the suffering of death crowned with glory and honor, that by the grace of God He might taste death for everyone."

God's holiness required the penalty of death for those guilty of sin. This meant all humanity. The justifiable wrath of God is directed against sin. It is directed against us when sin dwells in us. However, God in His mercy established a sacrificial means whereby His wrath could be diverted away from us toward a person who was willing to stand in our place. This person had to be without sin, acceptable to God, and willing to voluntarily die for our sins. This person was Jesus, who stated in John 10:17-18:

> "For this reason, the Father loves Me, because I lay down My life that I may take it up again. No one has taken it away from Me, but I lay it down on My own initiative. I have authority to lay it down, and I have authority to take it up again. This commandment I receive from My Father."

God's wrath was directed against Jesus when He shed His blood on a cross. Jesus was a propitiation for our sins; He stood in our place and accepted our death sentence for sin. John stated in 1 John 2:1-2:

> "My little children, I am writing these things to you so that you may not sin. And if anyone sins, we have an Advocate with the Father, Jesus Christ the righteous; and He Himself is the propitiation for our sins; and not for ours only, but also for those of the whole world."

Paul stated in Colossians 2:13-14:

> "And when you were dead in your transgressions and the uncircumcision of your flesh, He made you alive together with Him, having forgiven us all our transgressions, having canceled out the certificate of debt consisting of decrees against us and which was hostile to us; and He has taken it out of the way, having nailed it to the cross."

Jesus' holiness and obedience to God made it possible for His blood shed on a cross to be an acceptable sacrifice to cleanse us from our sins. John stated in 1 John 1:7:

> "If we walk in the light as He Himself is in the Light, we have fellowship with one another, and the blood of Jesus His Son cleanses us from all sin."

Jesus is our high priest in heaven. In Hebrews 4:15, 7:23-27, the author stated:

> "For we do not have a high priest who cannot sympathize with our weaknesses, but one who has been tempted in all things as we are, yet without sin. ... The former priests, on the one hand, existed in greater numbers because they were prevented by death from continuing, but He, on the other hand, because He abides forever, holds His priesthood permanently. Hence, also, He is able to save forever those who draw near to God through Him, since He always lives to make intercession for them. For it was fitting that we should have such a high priest, holy, innocent, undefiled, separated from sinners and exalted above the heavens; who does not need daily, like those high priest, to offer up sacrifices, first for his own sins, and then for the sins of the people, because this He did once for all when He offered up Himself."

Jesus understands our weaknesses because He has been tempted like us. He holds His priesthood forever and continually intercedes for us before His Father.

Genesis indicates God created men and women to have and exercise dominion over His creation. However, this dominion was transferred to Satan when Adam disobeyed God and sinned. Even though we may not intentionally serve Satan, we all experience the consequences of this transfer.

Jewish law in Leviticus 25:25 states:

> "If a fellow countryman of yours becomes so poor he has to sell part of his property, then his nearest kinsman is to come and buy back what his relative has sold."

A Jew and his property could only be redeemed by a kinsman who was a blood relative and willing to pay his debt when he sold himself into bondage to pay his debt.

Adam's disobedience and sin in the Garden of Eden placed him and all humanity into bondage to Satan and transferred dominion to him. Therefore, only a person who could act as our kinsman could pay the ransom to redeem us from this bondage and return to us the dominion God originally gave us. This person had to have the authority to carry out the required transaction to pay this ransom. He had to be perfectly obedient to God and without sin because Adam's disobedience and sin brought us into bondage to Satan. This person would have to be born into this world to have the authority to pay the ransom. This was accomplished by Jesus being born into this world through the seed of God being implanted in the womb of a virgin.

Jesus was our kinsman who had the authority to pay the ransom. Jesus' death, which satisfied the justifiable wrath of God against our sins, was the acceptable ransom to redeem us from bondage to Satan and return God's dominion to us when He died on a cross. Jesus stated in Mark 20:45:

> "For even the Son of Man did not come to be served, but to serve, and to give His life a ransom for many."

Paul stated in 1 Timothy 2:5-6

> "For there is one God, and one mediator also between God and men, the man Christ Jesus, who gave Himself as a ransom for all, the testimony borne at the proper time."

In Hebrews 2:14-15, the author stated:

> "Since then the children share in flesh and blood, He Himself likewise also partook of the same, that through death He might render powerless him who had the power of death, that is the devil; and might deliver those who through fear were subject to slavery all their lives."

Jesus' sacrificial death rendered Satan's power over death powerless and ended his dominion over us. Jesus has removed the obstacles that stood between God and us. He replaced the Law that could only convict us of sin and bring death to us with a new covenant that reconciles us to God and gives us eternal life through Him. Jesus voluntarily accepted God's death penalty for our sins by dying on a cross in our place. He was the acceptable ransom to redeem us from our bondage to Satan and end his dominion over us. Jesus is our eternal high priest in heaven who is there to intercede to God for us. Therefore, when we approach God through Jesus, He no longer sees our sin natures; He sees us in the light of the righteousness of His Son, Jesus. Paul stated in Romans 8:9-10:

> "However, you are not in the flesh but in the Spirit, if indeed the Spirit of God dwells in you. But if anyone does not have the Spirit of Christ, he does not belong to Him. And if Christ is in you, though the body is dead because of sin, yet the spirit is alive because of righteousness."

We are made spiritually alive when we come into the presence of God, the Father, through Jesus, His Son, and receive the Holy Spirit into our heart, so we can fellowship and commune with Them.

Jesus came to send the Holy Spirit into the world. He stated in John 14:16-18:

> "I will ask the Father, and He will give you another Helper, that He may be with you forever, that is the Spirit of Truth, whom the world cannot receive, because it does not see Him or know Him, but you know Him because He abides with you and will be in you."

Jesus promised His disciples He would not leave them orphans or defenseless. He indicated the Holy Spirit would give them remembrance of all He had taught them. Jesus continued in John 16:7-11:

> "But I tell you the truth, it is to your advantage that I go away; for if I do not go away, the Helper will not come to you; but if I go, I will send Him to you. And He, when He comes, will convict the world concerning sin and righteousness and judgment; concerning sin, because they do not believe in

Me; and concerning righteousness, because I go to the Father and you no longer see Me; and concerning judgement, because the ruler of this world has been judged."

The Holy Spirit gave the disciples the ability to proclaim repentance for sin, preach the gospel of Jesus, witness to the presence of Jesus in their lives, and make disciples of others. When we accept Jesus as our Lord and Savior and invite the Holy Spirit, He dwells within us and gives us these same abilities.\

OUR RELATIONSHIP WITH GOD THROUGH JESUS

Entering the Kingdom of God through Our Faith in Jesus

Jesus stated in Matthew 18:3:

> "Truly I say to you, unless you are converted and become like children, you will not enter the kingdom of heaven."

We must turn from our love of the world to Jesus with a childlike faith to enter a relationship with God through Him. Jesus then stated in John 3:5-6:

> "Truly, truly, I say to you, unless one is born of water and the Spirit he cannot enter into the kingdom of God. That which is born of the flesh is flesh, and that which is born of the Spirit is spirit."

We must be spiritually reborn to enter the kingdom of God.
  Peter stated in Acts 3:19, 4:12:

> "Therefore repent and return, so that your sins may be wiped away, in order that times of refreshing may come from the presence of the Lord." … And there is salvation in no one else; for there is no other name under heaven that has been given among men by which we must be saved."

We receive God's redemption only through our faith in Jesus. We must approach God with a repentant heart. Repentance is an act of regret and remorse for living a life of sin apart from God. Jesus stated in Luke 13:3, "but unless you repent, you will all likewise perish." He then stated in Luke 15:7:

> "There will be more joy in heaven over one sinner who repents, than over ninety-nine righteous persons who need no repentance."

God forgives us and begins the process of regenerating and transforming us through the Holy Spirit in our life when we repent and approach Him through Jesus.

We must understand the relation between the Law of Moses and God's redemption that we receive through our faith in Jesus. Paul stated in Romans 3:19-26:

> "Now we know that whatever the Law says, it speaks to those who are under the Law, so that every mouth may be closed and all the world may become accountable to God; because by the works of the Law no flesh will be justified in His sight, for through the Law comes the knowledge of sin. But now apart from the Law the righteousness of God has been manifested, being witnessed by the Law and the Prophets, even the righteousness of God through faith in Jesus Christ for all those who believe; for there is no distinction; for all have sinned and fall short of the glory of God, being justified as a gift by His grace through the redemption which is in Christ Jesus; whom God displayed publicly as a propitiation in His blood through faith. This was to demonstrate His righteousness, because in the forbearance of God He passed over the sins previously committed; for the demonstration, I say, of His righteousness at the present time, so that He would be just and the justifier of the one who has faith in Jesus."

We are guilty of sins that separate us from God. The Law only gives us knowledge of our sins by defining them. It then convicts us of our sins and holds us accountable before God. As a result, the works of the Law cannot justify us before God. They cannot declare us to be innocent of our sins nor can they redeem and reconcile us to Him. Therefore, we need a Savior, Jesus, who can be a propitiation for our sins. He took our place on a cross and received God's death penalty for our sins. We are justified through Jesus' sacrificial death and declared to be innocent by the gift of God's grace. This grace is extended to us when we accept by faith the redemption and reconciliation, we receive through the blood of Jesus that God publicly displayed on a cross.

Jesus stated in John 14:6, "I am the way, and the truth, and the life; no one comes to the Father but through Me." We enter a reconciled relationship with God through Jesus by following Paul's instructions in Romans 10:8-10:

> "But what does it say? 'The word is near you, in your mouth and in your heart' (Deuteronomy 30:14) - that is, the word of faith which we are preaching,

that if you confess with your mouth Jesus as Lord, and believe in your heart that God raised Him from the dead, you will be saved; for with the heart a person believes, resulting in righteousness, and with the mouth he confesses, resulting in salvation."

The Holy Spirit creates the desire in our heart and gives us the ability through our mind to believe in and trust Jesus when He convicts us of sin. This enables us to publicly confess with our mouth Jesus is Lord. Righteousness is then accredited to us through Jesus as our heart is transformed by the Holy Spirit, and our salvation is assured when we confess Jesus is Lord.

Paul further stated in Ephesians 2:8-10:

"For by grace you have been saved through faith and that not of yourselves. It is the gift of God; not as a result of works, so that no one may boast. For we are His workmanship, created in Christ Jesus for good works, which God prepared beforehand so that we would walk in them."

Paul reaffirmed the salvation we receive through our faith in Jesus is a gift from God. We cannot boast that we have earned or deserve our salvation based on our own merit or efforts. We can only receive it as a gift extended to us by God. Paul indicated we have been created in Jesus to do good works even though we are not saved by good works.

Spiritual Growth and Maturity in Our Relationship with Jesus

Jesus becomes our Savior and the Lord of our life when we enter our relationship with God through Him. He restores our broken relationship with God caused by sin in our life as our Savior. We then need to allow Him to become ruler and master of all areas in our life, not just areas we select, as Lord of our life. Areas in our life where Jesus becomes Lord are determined by our life choices and actions after we receive Him as our Savior. Our relationship with Jesus as our Savior is impaired when areas remain in our life where we have not allowed Him to be Lord. However, Jesus restores impaired areas in our relationship with Him as our Savior when we repent, ask Him to forgive us, and allow Him to be the Lord of these areas in our life.

We need to internalize God's word in the Bible to grow in our relationship with Jesus as Lord of our life. The Holy Spirit then facilitates our spiritual growth and maturity through His presence in our life. Paul emphasized the importance of our internalizing God's word in the Bible when he stated in 2 Timothy 3:16-17:

"All Scripture is inspired by God and profitable for teaching, for reproof, for correction, for training in righteousness; that the man of God may be adequate, equipped for every good work."

Peter instructed us after we enter our relationship with Jesus in 1 Peter 2:1-3:

"Therefore, putting aside all malice and all deceit and hypocrisy and envy and all slander, like newborn babes, long for the pure milk of the word, so that by it you may grow in respect to salvation if you have tasted the kindness of the Lord."

We are to "grow in respect to [our] salvation" by reading, studying and internalizing God's word in the Bible when we receive the salvation He extends to us through Jesus.
    Paul further instructed us in Philippians 2:12-13:

"So then, my beloved, just as you have always obeyed, not as in my presence only, but now much more in my absence, work out your salvation with fear and trembling, for it is God who is at work in you, both to will and to work for His good pleasure."

Paul indicated we are to work out our salvation even though the redemption and salvation we receive from God through Jesus is a gift. We do this by growing in our ability to live a life of faith and trust in and obedience to God and Jesus through the presence of the Holy Spirit in our life. This growth is accomplished through faithful and disciplined Bible study essential for us to:

- Learn and internalize God's spiritual life principles revealed in the Bible;
- Experience the resulting renewing of our mind and transforming of our heart through actions of the Holy Spirit in our life as we internalize these spiritual life principles; and
- Learn and take advantage of God's covenant promises available to us because of our relationship with Him through Jesus.

Paul indicated in 2 Timothy 3:16-17 our knowledge of the Scriptures more effectively equips us to live a life of obedience to God and makes it possible for Him "to will and to work for His good pleasure" through us.
    Paul stated in 1 Corinthians 3:9-15:

> "For we are God's fellow workers; you are God's field, God's building. According to the grace of God which was given to me, like a wise master builder I laid a foundation, and another is building on it. But each man must be careful how he builds on it. For no man can lay a foundation other than the one which is laid, which is Jesus Christ. Now if any man builds on the foundation with gold, silver, precious stones, wood, hay, straw, each man's work will become evident; for the day will show it because it is to be revealed with fire, and the fire itself will test the quality of each man's work. If any man's work is burned up, he will suffer loss; but he himself will be saved, yet so as through fire."

Jesus must be the foundation of our life on which we continue to build as we grow in our faith, spiritually mature, and perform good works God prepares and places before us. Our motives for performing our good works and their quality will be revealed and tested by fire when Jesus examines them on the last day. Some will be accepted by Him and remain. Others may be rejected and burned up. We will suffer loss for those good works that are rejected, but we will not lose our salvation.

Jesus affirmed the importance of Him being the foundation of our life on which we continue to build when He stated in John 15:1-6:

> "I am the true vine, and My Father is the vine dresser. Every branch in Me that does not bear fruit, He takes away; and every branch that bears fruit, He prunes it so that it may bear more fruit. You are already clean because of the word which I have spoken to you. Abide in Me, and I in you. As the branch cannot bear fruit of itself unless it abides in the vine, so neither can you unless you abide in Me. I am the vine, you are the branches; he who abides in Me and I in him, he bears much fruit, for apart from Me you can do nothing. If anyone does not abide in Me, he is thrown away as a branch and dries up; and they gather them, and cast them into the fire and they are burned."

Jesus indicated:

- We are to grow, mature and bear fruit in our relationship with Him;
- We will not be able to do these independent of Him; and
- God will remove us from our relationship with Him when we fail to grow, mature and bear fruit in this relationship.

Jesus' warning is often overlooked or ignored, but it is consistent with similar warnings He gave us in His parables of the talents in Mathew 25:14-30 and Luke 19:12-27. Jesus affirmed God will enable and equip us to bear more fruit as we grow and mature in our relationship with Him.

Peter stated in 2 Peter 1:5-11:

> "Now for this very reason also, applying all diligence, in your faith supply moral excellence, and in your moral excellence, knowledge; and in your knowledge, self-control, and in your self-control, perseverance, and in your perseverance, godliness; and in your godliness, brotherly kindness, and in your brotherly kindness, love. For if these qualities are yours and are increasing, they render you neither useless nor unfruitful in the true knowledge of our Lord Jesus Christ. For he who lacks these qualities is blind or shortsighted, having forgotten his purification from his former sins. Therefore, brethren, be all the more diligent to make certain about His calling and choosing you; for as long as you practice these things, you will never stumble; for in this wway the entrance into the eternal kingdom of our Lord and Savior Jesus Christ will be abundantly supplied to you."

Peter's progression results from God's pruning transforms our faith into genuine love we can share with and extend to others without expecting something in return. Faith and trust in God, Jesus and the Holy Spirit precede and result in moral excellence. Moral excellence facilitates the acquisition of spiritual knowledge. Spiritual knowledge enables self-control. Self-control facilitates perseverance. Perseverance results in godliness. Godliness leads to brotherly kindness. Brotherly kindness results in genuine love. This progression enables and equips us to bear fruit as we spiritually grow, mature and engage in the good works God has prepared for us to perform. It assures our entrance into Jesus' eternal kingdom. Jesus instructed us in Matthew 5:16:

> "Let your light shine before men in such a way that they may see your good works, and glorify your Father who is in heaven."

Four Stages of Spiritual Growth

God requires us to spiritually grow and mature when we enter our relationship with Him through Jesus. We are to study, internalize and assimilate the solid food in the Bible. Spiritual growth, like physical and emotional growth, progresses through the four stages of infancy, childhood, adolescence and adulthood. The characteristics of each stage can be summarized with a two-word phrase: infancy - *feed me*, childhood - *teach me*, adolescence - *guide me*, and adulthood - *use me*.

Spiritual Infancy: We have no or little knowledge of God's word presented in the Bible during spiritual infancy. Therefore, God does not expect us to have this knowledge during spiritual infancy nor does He hold us accountable for our disobedience to Him and Jesus because we lack this knowledge. The development of our understanding of the Bible and our spiritual growth is influenced by the knowledge and integrity of Christians with whom we fellowship as spiritual infants. Therefore, we must be in an environment where we can be fed the pure milk of God's word and be protected from influences that will draw us away from God and Jesus as we begin our spiritual growth. This environment is present in a Christian church where we are taught God's unaltered word from the Bible and hear His word preached from the pulpit.

Spiritual Childhood: We enter spiritual childhood as we continue to feed on the pure milk of God's word in the Bible and begin to incorporate its precepts into our life. We are to grow in our knowledge and understanding of God's word in the Bible during spiritual childhood. We develop spiritual perspectives and life skills as we study the Bible and observe how spiritually mature Christians have incorporate biblical precepts into their lives. We often do not develop the spiritual maturity necessary to engage in the good works God has prepared for us during spiritual childhood even though we grow spiritually.

Spiritual Adolescence: We enter spiritual adolescence as our spiritual growth continues. This is often a difficult, troubled and rebellious time during our spiritual growth. We discover our desires and lifestyle conflict with our knowledge of God's word, and we must make changes in our life as we move closer to God through Jesus. These changes are often difficult to make and require we enter mentoring relationships with mature Christians we trust and with whom we can share sensitive and personal life issues. Our knowledge of God's word and related spiritual perspectives become convictions that form our character as we work through and make these life changes. We discover God's word is true and God is faithful to honor His word. We begin to develop spiritual maturity necessary to enable and equip us to perform the good works God has prepared for us as we progress through spiritual adolescence.

Spiritual Adulthood: We enter spiritual adulthood as we spiritually grow and develop spiritual maturity. These are lifelong processes that progress as we feed on and digest the solid food of God's word in the Bible. We become spiritual adults as we develop the ability to decern the differences between good and evil. We are then equipped to engage in the good works God has prepared for us.

The Relation between Faith, Grace and Good Works

Grace and faith are the foundation of our relationship with God through Jesus. He redeems and reconciles us through His grace. However, He requires us to enter the good works He calls us to enter. These good works are the ministries and service to others God calls us to enter in Jesus' name.

Many who understand the significance of grace and faith in our relationship with God through Jesus do not understand the significance of good works in this relationship. Two scripture verses help us understand the relation between grace, faith and good works. The first is Ephesians 2:8-10, where Paul stated:

> "For by grace you have been saved through faith and that not of yourselves. It is the gift of God; not as a result of works, so that no one may boast. For we are His workmanship, created in Christ Jesus for good works, which God prepared beforehand so that we would walk in them."

The second is James 2:14-26 where James stated:

> "What use is it my brethren, if a man says he has faith, but he has no works? Can that faith save him? If a brother or sister is without clothing and in need of daily food, and one of you says to them, 'Go in peace, be warmed and be filled,' and yet you do not give them what is necessary for their body, what use is that? Even so faith, if it has no works, is dead, being by itself. But someone may well say, 'You have faith, and I have works; show me your faith without works, and I will show you my faith by my works.' You believe that God is one. You do well; the demons also believe, and shudder. But are you willing to recognize, you foolish fellow, that faith without works is useless? Was not Abraham our father justified by works, when he offered up Isaac his son on the altar? You see that a man is justified by works, and not by faith alone. And in the same way was not Rahab the harlot also justified by works, when she received the messengers and sent them out by another way? For just as the body without the spirit is dead, so also faith without works is dead."

There are two types of works referred to in these scripture verses. The first type of works are works referred to in Ephesians 2:8 that we use to justify ourself to God. Paul indicated these works will never justify us to God. The second type of works referred to in Ephesians 2:10 are "good works, which God prepared beforehand so that we would walk in them."

It is reasonable to belief the works referred to in James 2:17-26 are the same as the good works referred to in Ephesians 2:10.

Paul indicated in Ephesians 2:8 we are redeemed by God's grace through Jesus. James and Paul taught our faith in Jesus must result in our love for and obedience to Him. Our faith must motivate us to perform the good works God has prepared beforehand for us to perform. James stated our faith becomes useless and dies when we do not enter these good works. Our relationship with God is impaired when we do not live a life of faith and trust in and obedience to Jesus. Our faith dies when it does not motivate us to perform good works the Holy Spirit leads us to perform.

Four Responses to God's Word

Jesus stated in Matthew 7:13-14:

> "Enter through the narrow gate; for the gate is wide and the way is broad that leads to destruction, and there are many who enter through it. For the gate is small and the way is narrow that leads to life, and there are few who find it."

The Bible teaches we must:

- Study and internalize God's word in the Bible (1 Peter 2:1-3),
- Build our life on the foundation of Jesus (1 Corinthians 3:9-15), and
- Enter and perform the good works God has prepared for us to walk in (Ephesians 2:8-10).

These enable us to grow and mature in our relationship with God through Jesus. This requires commitment and perseverance to overcome the challenges, obstacles and hardships we will experience as a result of this relationship. Many who initially enter a relationship with God through Jesus lack this commitment and perseverance.

Jesus addressed this in His parable of the Sower in Matthew 13:3-9, 18-23. He indicated in Matthew 13:3-9 the spreading of God's word can be visualized as a sower spreading seeds. "Some seeds fell beside the road, and the birds came and ate them up." Other seeds fell on rocky places where they had insufficient soil in which to grow and immediately began to grow. Because they lacked depth of soil and roots, "when the sun had risen, they were scorched; and … they withered away." Other seeds fell among thorns, and "the thorns came up and choked them out." Other seeds "fell on the good soil and yielded a crop, some a hundredfold, some sixty and some thirty."

Jesus explained His parable in Matthew 13:18-23. He indicated:

- **Seeds that fall beside the road:** These seeds represent those who do not understand God's word when they hear it. Satan snatches it from their heart when this occurs.

- **Seeds that fall on rocky places:** These seeds represent those who initially receive God's word with joy when they hear it. However, they do not study and internalize God's word in the Bible. As a result, their faith is shallow, and they do not build their life on the foundation of Jesus. Therefore, they fall away when they experience affliction, persecution and hard times because of God's word.

- Seeds that fall among thorns: These seeds represent those who hear, study and internalize God's word in the Bible. They begin to build their life on the foundation of Jesus. However, the concerns of the world and the deceitfulness of wealth take root in their heart and grow. Eventually, these choke out God's word in their heart, and they fall away from God.

- **Seeds that fall on the good soil:** These seeds represent those who hear, study and internalize God's word in the Bible and who build their life on the foundation of Jesus. God's word bears much fruit in their life. Some bring forth a hundredfold, some sixty and some thirty.

In Hebrews 10:26-31, the author stated:

> "For if we go on sinning willfully after receiving the knowledge of the truth, there no longer remains a sacrifice for sins, but a terrifying expectation of judgement and the fury of a fire which will consume the adversary. (Isaiah 26:11) Anyone who has set aside the Law of Moses dies without mercy on the testimony of two or three witnesses. (Deuteronomy 17:6) How much severer punishment do you think he will deserve who has trampled underfoot the Son of God, and has regarded as unclean the blood of the covenant by which he was sanctified, and has insulted the Spirit of grace? For we know Him who said, 'Vengeance is mine, I will repay.' Deuteronomy 32:35 And again, 'The LORD will judge His people.' (Deuteronomy 32:36) It is a terrifying thing to fall into the hands of the living God."

This Bible verse describes those who hear and receive God's word and continue in a life of willful sin. They are deceived by Satan into believing this is okay. The writer of Hebrews stated those who do this will have the "terrifying expectation of judgment." These individuals are represented by the Sower's seeds that fall beside the road.

Peter stated in 2 Peter 2:20-21:

> "For if, after they have escaped the defilement of the world by the knowledge of the Lord and Savior Jesus Christ, they are again entangled in them and are overcome, the last state has become worse for them than the firs. For it would be better for them not to have known the way of righteousness, than having known it, to turn away from the holy commandment handed on to them."

This Bible verse describes those who hear and receive God's word, but they do not study and internalize it and begin to build their life on the foundation of Jesus. As a result, they are drawn back into and entangled in the life of sin they left. Peter indicated the state of sin they reenter will be worse than the state of sin they left. These individuals are represented by the Sower's seeds that fall on rocky places.

In Hebrews 6:4-6, the author stated:

> "For in the case of those who have once been enlightened and have tasted of the heavenly gift and have been made partakers of the Holy Spirit, and have tasted the good word of God and the power of the ages to come, and then have fallen away, it is impossible to renew them again to repentance, since they again crucify to themselves the Son of God and put Him to open sham."

This Bible verse describes those who hear and receive God's word, study and internalize it, and begin to build their life on the foundation of Jesus. The concerns of the world and the deceitfulness of wealth then take root and grow in their heart. They eventually choke our God's word in the life of these individuals, and they abandon their relationship with God. The writer of Hebrews stated it will be "impossible to renew them again to repentance" when this occurs. These individuals are represented by the Sower's seeds that fall among thorns.

The fourth group of the Sower's seeds represents those who love and are obedient to Jesus. They have entered a relationship with God through Him. They study and internalize God's word in the Bible. They build their life on the foundation of Jesus. They enter and perform the good works God prepares for them. They demonstrate their love for, faith in and obedience to Jesus by keeping His commandments and His words. Jesus stated in John 14:15, 21 and 23:

> "If you love Me, you will keep My commandments. ... He who has My commandments and keeps them is the one who loves Me, and he who loves

Me will be loved by My Father, and I will love him and will disclose Myself to him. ... If anyone loves Me, he will keep My word; and My Father will love him, and We will come to him and make Our abode with him."

Reciprocal actions on the part of those who love and are obedient to Jesus and on the parts of God and Jesus are revealed in this scripture. Individuals who love and are obedient to Jesus demonstrate their love by keeping His commandments and words, and they demonstrate their love and obedience by their good works and their life choices and actions. Both God and Jesus reciprocate by loving them, disclosing Themselves to them, and taking up residence in them. The more of themselves these individuals yield in trust in and obedience to God and Jesus the more of Themselves will They disclose to them through the Holy Spirit. As a result, God's word bears much fruit in their lives, yielding a hundredfold in some and sixty and thirty folds in others.

Security of Our Relationship with God through Jesus

Our relationship with God through Jesus is secure. Paul stated in Romans 8:35-39:

> "Who will separate us from the love of Christ? Will tribulation, or distress, or persecution, or famine, or nakedness, or peril, or sword? Just as it is written, 'For your sake we are being put to death all day long, we were considered as sheep to be slaughtered.' (Psalms 44:22) But in all these things we overwhelmingly conquer through Him who loved us. For I am convinced that neither death, nor life, nor angels, nor principalities, nor things present, nor things to come, nor powers, nor height, nor depth, nor any other created thing, will be able to separate us from the love of God, which is in Christ Jesus."

Nothing in all creation will be able to separate us from the love of God extended to us through Jesus. Jesus confirmed the security of our relationship with God through Him when He stated in John 3:16-18.

> "For God so loved the world, that He gave His only begotten Son, that whoever believes in Him shall not perish, but have eternal life. For God did not send the Son into the world to judge the world, but that the world might be saved through Him. He who believes in Him is not judged; he who does not believe has been judged already, because he has not believed in the name of the only begotten Son of God."

He continued in John 6:35-40:

> "I am the bread of life; he who comes to Me will not hunger, and he who believes in Me will never thirst. But I said to you that you have seen Me, and yet do not believe. All that the Father gives Me will come to Me, and the one who comes to Me I will certainly not cast out. For I have come down from heaven, not to do My own will, but the will of Him who sent Me. This is the will of Him who sent Me, that of all that He has given Me I lose nothing, but raise it up on the last day. For this is the will of My Father, that everyone who beholds the Son and believes in Him will have eternal life, and I Myself will raise him up on the last day."

and in John 10:27-30:

> "My sheep hear My voice, and I know them, and they follow Me; and I give eternal life to them, and they will never perish; and no one will snatch them out of My hand. My Father, who has given them to Me, is greater than all; and no one is able to snatch them out of the Father's hand. I and the Father are one."

Closing Comments

In Hebrews 9:27-28, the author stated regarding our salvation through Jesus:

> "And inasmuch as it is appointed for men to die once and after this comes judgment, so Christ also, having been offered once to bear the sins of many, will appear a second time for salvation without reference to sin, to those who eagerly await Him."

We experience judgement immediately after we die because Jesus' death and resurrection did not do away with the Law even though they fulfilled it. The Law defines and convicts us of our sins. Therefore, it declares us guilty of our sins before the judgement seat of God when we have not sought nor received God's salvation through Jesus before we die. This declaration eternally separates us from God, Jesus and the Holy Spirit. The barrier of our sins that separates us from Them is only removed when we seek and have received God's salvation though Jesus before we die. It is not possible to seek God's salvation through Jesus after we die.

Paul stated in Romans 8:15-17:

"For you have not received a spirit of slavery leading to fear again, but you have received a spirit of adoption as sons by which we cry out, 'Abba! Father!' The Spirit Himself testifies with our spirit that we are children of God, and if children, heirs also, heirs of God and fellow heirs with Christ, if indeed we suffer with Him so that we may also be glorified with Him."

We become God's adopted children when we enter a reconciled relationship with Him through our faith and trust in and obedience to Jesus, and we grow and mature in this relationship through the indwelling presence of the Holy Spirit. We are fellow heirs with Jesus with the rights and privileges of being heirs of God.

CHAPTER 7
JUDGMENTS OF GOD

GOD'S FIXED DAY FOR JUDGMENT

Paul stated in Acts 17:30-31:

> "Therefore having overlooked the times of ignorance, God is now declaring to men that all people everywhere should repent, because He has fixed a day in which He will judge the world in righteousness through a Man whom He has appointed, having furnished proof to all men by raising Him from the dead."

God has "fixed a day in which He will Judge the world" through His Son, Jesus. We normally think in terms of a life span of 80 - 90 years. This governs the life choices we make and the characters we develop. We must think in terms of eternity when we address the judgments of God through Jesus. The positions the unrighteous and righteous with God, Jesus and the Holy Spirit will be fixed forever after they have been judged by Jesus. They will never change. The unrighteous will be separated from God, Jesus and the Holy Spirit in the lake of fire forever. The positions of the righteous in the kingdom of heaven will be fixed forever.

JESUS' CRITERIA FOR JUDGMENT

Jesus stated at the beginning of His ministry in Matthew 5:17-19:

> "Do not think that I came to abolish the Law or the Prophets; I did not come to abolish but to fulfill. For truly I say to you, until heaven and earth pass away, not the smallest letter or stroke shall pass from the Law until all is accomplished. Whoever then annuls one of the least of these commandments, and teaches others to do the same, shall be called least in the kingdom of heaven; but whoever keeps and teaches them, he shall be called great in the kingdom of heaven."

Jesus addressed three major points in His statement. First, He came to fulfill the Law and Prophets, not do away with them. Second, nothing shall be removed from or changed in the Law until heaven and earth pass away. This will not occur until just before the great white throne judgment the unrighteous will experience after the completion of Jesus' 1,000-year kingdom (Revelation 20:11, 21:1-2). Third, Jesus indicated the righteous who enter the kingdom of heaven will be separated into two groups. The righteous who have changed one of the least of the commandments of the Law and have taught others to do the same shall be called least in the kingdom of heaven, while the righteous who have obeyed and taught them to others shall be called great in the kingdom of heaven. Jesus' statement indicated God's grace and redemption will apply to the righteous who have changed one of the least of the commandments of the Law and have taught others to do the same. However, their position in the kingdom of heaven will be different from the righteous who have obeyed the commandments of the Law and have taught them to others.

Jesus presented the criteria we will be judged by. He stated in John 12:48-49:

> "He who rejects Me and does not receive My sayings, has one who judges him; the word I spoke is what will judge him at the last day. For I did not speak on My own initiative, but the Father Himself who sent Me has given Me a commandment as to what to say and what to speak."

Jesus stated in John 14:23, "If anyone loves Me, he will keep My word." John stated in 2 John 1:8-9:

> "Watch yourselves, that you do not lose what we have accomplished, but that you may receive a full reward. Anyone who goes too far and does not abide in the teaching of Christ, does not have God; the one who abides in the teaching, he has both the Father and the Son."

The unrighteous who have not abided in the teaching of Jesus have rejected God. Therefore, their names will not be written in the book of life. They will be judged and thrown into the lake of fire when they stand before Jesus at the great white throne judgment. However, the righteous who have been faithful to and abided in the teaching of Jesus will have "both the Father and Son," and their names will be written in the book of life. They will "receive a full reward" for the good works they have done in Jesus' name when they stand before Him. More will be said about this later.

Jesus addressed the judgment of the righteous and unrighteous in Matthew 25:31-46. He stated:

"But when the Son of Man comes in His glory, and all the angels with Him, then He will sit on His glorious throne. All the nations will be gathered before Him; and He will separate them one from another, as the shepherd separates the sheep from the goats, and He will put the sheep on His right, and the goats on the left."

"Then the King will say to those on His right, 'Come, you who are blessed of My Father, inherit the kingdom prepared for you from the foundation of the world. For I was hungry, and you gave Me something to eat; I was thirsty, and you gave Me something to drink; I was a stranger, and you invited Me in; naked, and you clothed Me; I was sick, and you visited Me; I was in prison, and you came to Me.' Then the righteous will answer Him, 'Lord, when did we see You hungry, and feed You, or thirsty, and give You something to drink? And when did we see You a stranger, and invite You in, or naked, and clothe You? When did we see You sick, or in prison, and come to You?' The King will answer and say to them, 'Truly I say to you, to the extent that you did it to one of these brothers of Mine, even the least of them, You did it to Me."

"Then He will also say to those on His left, 'Depart from Me, accursed ones, into the eternal fire which has been prepared for the devil and his angels; for I was hungry, and you gave Me nothing to eat; I was thirst, and you gave Me nothing to drink; I was a stranger, and you did not invite Me in; naked, and you did not clothe Me; sick, and in prison, and you did not visit Me.' Then they themselves also will answer, 'Lord, when did we see You hungry, or thirsty, or a stranger, or naked, or sick, or in prison, and did not take care of You?' Then He will answer them, 'Truly I say to you, to the extent that you did not do it to one of the least of these, you did not do it to Me.' These will go away into eternal punishment, but the righteous into eternal life."

Jesus will separate those who have performed works in His name as a shepherd separates sheep from goats when He returns. Sheep conjugate in flocks with a shepherd who protects, cares for, leads, and keeps them from straying from the flock. Goats gather in herds with a herdsman who cares for them. Goats are more independent than sheep and are by nature curious and often stray into new and unfamiliar areas. Sheep represent individuals who seek Jesus to lead and guide them through the presence of the Holy Spirit in their lives as they study, lean and internalize His words in the Gospels. Goats represent individuals with independent attitudes who stray from Jesus' words in the Gospels to follow beliefs His words do not confirm or support.

Jesus is our good shepherd who protects, cares for and leads us (John 10:11). He is also the Light of life and the Light of the world who guides us (John 8:12). Those who love and follow Jesus have the Light of life who enables them to walk in the Light of the world. He leads and guides them through the presence of the Holy Spirit in their lives as they grow and mature in their relationship with Him. This equips them to perform good works in His name that honor and glorify God, His Father. Jesus will receive them into His presence when He returns.

Those who stray from Jesus' words in the Gospels often walk in darkness, and they often perform works in His name that are motivated by beliefs His words in the Gospels do not confirm or support. These works may not honor and glorify God. Mainline liberal protestant churches and denominations who support the LGBT agenda stray from Jesus' words in the Gospels. The LGBT agenda supports same sex and bisexual sexual relations between men and women, same sex marriages, and the right for individuals to change the gender with which they were born. The moral Law defines all sexual relations between men and women outside of marriage as sin. God stated in Genesis 2:18, 21-24 and Jesus affirmed in Matthew 19:4-6 that marriage is to be a union between a man and a woman as husband and wife.

God's and Jesus' words in the Bible are immutable. They will never change or pass away. Jesus stated in Matthew 24:35, "Heaven and earth will pass away, but My words will not pass away." He stated in John 12:48-50 we will be judged by His words in the Gospels. Jesus' words will judge and condemn those who deliberately choose to stray from them. He will remove from His presence those who have not repented and been forgiven for straying from His words when He returns.

Jesus stated in Matthew 6:1-7:

> "Beware of practicing your righteousness before men to be noticed by them; otherwise you have no reward with your Father who is in heaven."
>
> "So when you give to the poor, do not sound a trumpet before you, as the hypocrites do in the synagogues and in the streets, so that they may be honored by men. Truly I say to you, they have their reward in full. But when you give to the poor, do not let your left hand know what your right hand is doing, so that your giving will be in secret; and your Father who sees what is done in secret will reward you."
>
> "When you pray, you are not to be like the hypocrites; for they love to stand and pray in the synagogues and on the street corners so that they may be seen by men. Truly I say to you, they have their reward in full. But you, when you pray, go into your inner room, close your door and pray to your Father who is in secret, and your Father who sees what is done in secret will reward you."

"And when you are praying, do not use meaningless repetition as the Gentiles do, for they suppose that they will be heard for their many words. So do not be like them; for your Father knows what you need before you ask Him."

We will be noticed and appreciated by others when these activities are motivated by our desire to be noticed and appreciated. Our reward will be being noticed and appreciated by others. However, we will not receive a reward from Jesus.

God expects us to grow in our knowledge of and internalize His word in the Bible and to enter and perform the good works He prepares for us to perform when we enter a relationship with Him through Jesus (Ephesians 2:10). Jesus indicated we show our love for Him by obeying His commandments and keeping His word (John 14:15, 21, 23). Our love for and obedience to Jesus is the foundation on which we build our life and develop our character. These must motivate us to enter the ministries and service to others we do in Jesus' name. He stated in Matthew 7:21-23:

"Not everyone who says to Me, 'Lord, Lord,' will enter the kingdom of heaven, but he who does the will of My Father who is in heaven will enter. Many will say to Me on that day, 'Lord, Lord, did we not prophesy in Your name, and in Your name cast out demons, and in Your name perform many miracles?' And then I will declare to them, 'I never knew you; depart from Me, you who practice lawlessness.' Psalms 6:8"

Jesus indicated not everyone who refer to Him as Lord and claim to perform works in His name will enter the kingdom of heaven. Only those who do the will of His Father will enter. We do the will of God when we receive and abide in the words of Jesus in the Gospels and obey His commandments. Jesus also indicated performing works in His name will not gain us entrance to the kingdom of heaven when we have intentional unrepentant sin in our life that we have not confessed and requested forgiven.

Jesus stated in a parable in Matthew 24:42-51, "the Son of Man is coming at an hour when you do not think He will." He then identified "the faithful and sensible slave whom his master put in charge of his household to give them their food at the proper time" as one "whom his master finds so doing when he comes." His master "will put him in charge of all his possessions" when he returns. Jesus identified the evil slave as one who believed "in his heart" his master will not return for a long time and who will begin "to beat his fellow slaves and eat and drink with drunkards." His master will "assign him to a place with the hypocrites" where "there will be weeping and gnashing of teeth" when he returns "on a day when he does not expect ... at an hour which he does not know." God expects us to perform good works He prepares for us to perform (Ephesians 2:10). We will receive our reward when our good works are examined by Jesus when we are properly motivated to perform them.

Jesus presented another parable in Matthew 25:1-13 in which He stated

> "The kingdom of heaven will be comparable to ten virgins, who took their lamps and went out to meet the bridegroom. Five of them were foolish, and five were prudent."

The foolish virgins took insufficient oil to keep their lamps lit when the bridegroom delayed his arrival. The prudent virgins took enough oil. The foolish virgins had to go and buy additional oil to keep their lamps lit when the bridegroom's arrival was delayed. While they were away, "the bridegroom came, and those who were ready went in with him to the wedding feast; and the door was shut." The foolish virgins asked, "Lord, lord, open up for us" when they arrived. The bridegroom stated, "Truly I say to you, I do not know you." It will be too late for us when we breathe our last breath and we have not entered a reconciled relationship with God through our faith in Jesus and accomplished the good works God has prepared for us to performs during our life. Jesus will tell us He does not know us when we stand before Him to examine our good works.

Jesus stated in Matthew 7:19-21:

> "Do not store up for yourselves treasures on earth, where moth and rust destroy, and where thieves break in and steal. But store up for yourselves treasures in heaven, where neither moth nor rust destroys, and where thieves do not break in or steal; for where your treasure is, there will your heart be also."

We build up and store for ourself treasures in heaven when we obey Jesus' words in the Gospels and perform the good works God prepares for us to perform. We will receive the treasures associated with our good works we have stored in heaven when we enter the kingdom of heaven.

Jesus continued in Matthew 7:24:

> "No one can serve two masters; for either he will hate the one and love the other, or he will be devoted to one and despise the other. You cannot serve God and wealth."

We must choose what motivates us as we make life choices and develop our character. Is it our love for and obedience to God, Jesus and the Holy Spirit, or is it our desire for wealth and the things of the world? The unrighteous who have rejected Jesus will be judged by what is written about them in the books that will be opened at the great white thrown judgment and thrown into the lake of fire. Those who claim they have but have not obeyed the words of Jesus in the Gospels and have only done their works to be noticed by others will be told by Jesus He does not know them, and they will be judged with the unrighteous. The righteous who have good works that are destroyed by fire when they are examined by Jesus will suffer loss and receive less than a full reward, and some will be called least in the kingdom of heaven. However, they will be there. The righteous who have faithfully been obedient to the words of Jesus in the Gospels and accomplished the good works God has prepared for them to perform will receive a full reward, and they will be called great in the kingdom of heaven.

JUDGMENT OF THE UNRIGHTEOUS AND RIGHTEOUS

Judgment of the Unrighteous - the Great White Throne Judgment

The great white throne judgment will occur at the end of Jesus' 1,000-year kingdom. John described this judgment in Revelation 20:11-15. He stated:

> "Then I saw a great white throne and Him who sat upon it, from whose presence earth and heaven fled away, and no place was found for them. And I saw the dead, the great and the small, standing before the throne, and books were opened; and another book was opened, which is the book of life; and the dead were judged from the things which were written in the books, according to their deeds. And the sea gave up the dead which were in it, and death and Hades gave up the dead which were in them; and they were judged, every one of them according to their deeds. Then death and Hades were thrown into the lake of fire. This is the second death, the lake of fire. And if anyone's name was not found written in the book of life, he was thrown into the lake of fire."

He who will sit on the great white throne is not identified. Jesus indicated in John 5:22-23 that God "has given judgement to the Son, so that all will honor the Son." Jesus will be the one who sits on the great white throne.

Everyone whose name is not written in the book of life will be judged according to what is written about them in the books that will be opened at the great white throne judgment. This will include the unrighteous who have rejected or not received Jesus as their Savior.

Their judgment will relate to what is written about them in the books that will be opened. They will be judged and sentenced to eternal separation from God, Jesus and the Holy Spirit in the lake of fire. God gives the unrighteous freedom to shape their lives and develop their characters by their life choices. They will experience the eternal consequences of their choices when Jesus judges them.

There will be three groups who will claim they were followers of Jesus who will be judged with the unrighteous and sentenced to eternal separation from God, Jesus and the Holy Spirit in the lake of fire. The first group will include those who during their lives after entering a relationship with Jesus have performed no good works as required by God in John 15:1-6, have completed none of the actions Peter outlined in 2 Peter 1:4-11, and have performed works solely for personal recognition and gain Jesus warned not to do in Matthew 6:1-6. Jesus will declare He does not know these individuals, and they will be sentenced to the lake of fire with the unrighteous.

The second group will be those who, after receiving the knowledge of the truth of God's word in the Bible, continue in a life of willful sin. In Hebrews 10:26-31, the author stated:

> "For if we go on sinning willfully after receiving the knowledge of the truth, there no longer remains a sacrifice for sins, but a terrifying expectation of judgment and the fury of a fire which will consume the adversary. (Isaiah 26:11) Anyone who has set aside the Law of Moses dies without mercy on the testimony of two or three witnesses. How much severer punishment do you think he will deserve who has trampled underfoot the Son of God, and has regarded as unclean the blood of the covenant by which he was sanctified, and has insulted the Spirit of grace? For we know Him who said, 'Vengeance is mine, I will repay.' (Deuteronomy 32:35) And again, 'The LORD will judge His people.' (Deuteronomy 32:36) It is a terrifying thing to fall into the hands of the living God."

The third group will be those who have accepted the redemption God offered them through Jesus and have internalized God's word in the Bible. However, they have allowed unforgiveness, bitterness, the concerns of the world, and their desire for wealth to take root and grow in their hearts. These eventually cause them to fall away from God and Jesus and reject the influence of the Holy Spirit in their lives. In Hebrews 6:4-6, the author stated when these occur:

> "For in the case of those who have once been enlightened and have tasted of the heavenly gift and have been made partakers of the Holy Spirit, and have tasted the good word of God and the power of the ages to come, and then have fallen away, it is impossible to renew them again to repentance, since they again crucify to themselves the Son of God and put Him to open shame."

Individuals in this group make a choice to reject God, Jesus and the Holy Spirit after receiving God's grace through Jesus and enlightenment from the Holy Spirit. The writer of Hebrews stated it will be "impossible to renew them again to repentance." They will be judged with the unrighteous and sentenced to the lake of fire.

The lake of fire will be where the unrighteous will experience the second death, which is eternal separation from God, Jesus and the Holy Spirit. This will be the eternal consequence of the deliberate choice they have made during their lives to reject God's provision for their redemption through His Son, Jesus. They will experience the second death because they have deliberately chosen to mock, dishonor and reject God.

Many do not understand why or accept the fact a loving God can and will condemn people to eternal separation from Him in the lake of fire. God brings us into the world for specific purposes and to fellowship and commune with Him. These purposes include accepting and receiving His love and grace for us through Jesus, loving and respecting Him in return, trusting Him and obeying His commandments and laws, and doing His will for their lives. These only have meaning when we have the freedom to choose whether or not to live our lives the way God desires. God will never force us to do anything we do not want to do, and He respects and honors the life choices we make. These are central to the human characteristics He creates within us. Therefore, He allows for the fact many will reject Him, His eternal values, and His purpose for their lives.

We start a slide away from God that will ultimately condemn us to eternal separation from Him, Jesus and the Holy Spirit when we deliberately choose to violate His commandments and laws, to mock, dishonor and reject Him, to do evil and worship other gods, etc. This is not God's choice for us; it is our choice that He honors. It is borne out by our consistently and deliberately choosing to live a life that rejects Him, His eternal values, and His Son, Jesus. Therefore, the eternal separation of the unrighteous from God in the lake of fire will be a continuation of the separation from Him they have consistently and deliberately chosen during their lives.

Dr. J. P. Morgan stated in Lee Stroble's book, *The Case for Faith* (2000):

> "Hell is not a place where people are consigned because they were pretty good blokes, but they just didn't believe the right stuff. They are consigned there, first and foremost, because they defy their maker and want to be at the center of the universe. Hell is not filled with people who have already repented, only God is not gentle enough or good enough to let them out. It's filled with people who, for all eternity, still want to be the center of the universe and who persist in their God-defying rebellion."

The position of the unrighteous will be sealed forever in the lake of fire after the great white throne judgment. It will never change. The messenger angel implied this in Daniel 12:2. Jesus indicated this in Matthew 25:41, 46. The angel indicated this to John in Revelation 14:11 and 20:10.

Judgment of the Righteous

The righteous will experience a judgment that is separate from the judgment of the unrighteous. Peter stated in 2 Peter 1:4-8, 10-11:

> "Now by these He has granted to us His precious and magnificent promises, so that by them you may become partakers of the divine nature, having escaped the corruption that is in the world by lust. Now for this very reason also, applying all diligence, in your faith supply moral excellence, and in your moral excellence, knowledge, and in your knowledge, self-control, and in your self-control, perseverance, and in your perseverance, godliness, and in your godliness, brotherly kindness, and in your brotherly kindness, love. For if these qualities are yours and are increasing, they render you neither useless nor unfruitful in the true knowledge of our Lord Jesus Christ. ... Therefore, brethren, be more diligent to make certain about His calling and choosing you; for as long as you practice these things, you will never stumble; for in this way the entrance into the eternal kingdom of our Lord and Savior Jesus Christ will be abundantly supplied to you."

Peter outlined the qualities we are to develop and display when we enter our relationship with God through our faith and trust in and obedience to Jesus and when we enter the "good works, which God prepared beforehand so that we would walk in them." (Ephesians 2:10) These qualities will render us "neither useless nor unfruitful in the true knowledge of our Lord Jesus Christ." God calls us to perform the good works He has specifically prepared for us to perform. With respect to our involvement in these good works, Paul stated in 2 Corinthians 5:10:

> "For we must all appear before the judgment seat of Christ, so that each one may be recompensed for his deeds in the body, according to what he has done, whether good or bad."

Jesus addressed the judgment the righteous will experience in the parable of the talents (Matthew 25:14-30). Jesus stated:

> "For it is just like a man about to go on a journey, who called his own slaves and entrusted his possessions to them. To one he gave five talents, to another two, and to another one, each according to his own ability; and he went on his journey."

A talent is a measure of weight. The Roman talent was 71 lb (32.3 kg). The value of 1 talent of gold today is around $1.3M and of 1 talent of silver is around $170K. The parable indicates the master expected his slaves to invest the talents he had entrusted to them. The slave who had received five talents earned five more talents. The slave who had received two talents earned two more talents. The slave who had received one talent buried his talent in the ground and earned nothing.

The master of the slaves after a long time came and settled accounts with them. The slaves who had received five and two talents showed him their gains of five and two talents. Their master said to them:

> "Well done, good and faithful slave. You were faithful with a few things, I will put you in charge of many things; enter into the joy of your master."

The slave who had received and buried the one talent appeared before his master with no gain. His master said to him:

> "You wicked, lazy slave ... you ought to have put my money in the bank and on my arrival I would have received my money back with interest. Therefore, take away the talent from him, and give it to the one who has the ten talents."

Then the master said:

> "For to everyone who has, more shall be given, and he will have an abundance, but from the one who does not have, even what he does have shall be taken away. Throw out the worthless slave into the outer darkness; in that place there will be weeping and gnashing of teeth."

The master's response in this parable is consistent with Jesus' statement in John 15:2 where He indicated those who are in a relationship with Him that do not bear fruit in the relationship will be removed from the relationship by God (John 15:1-2).

God apposes us when we are only motivated by acquiring wealth. He presents us with opportunities to acquire wealth when we have a proper attitude toward it.

He requires us to use a portion of the wealth we acquire to support good works He calls us and others to perform in return. He blesses us by providing opportunities for us to acquire more when we are faithful to do this. He may take our wealth from us when we inappropriately and selfishly use it.

Jesus used the proper investment of wealth in His parable of the talents (Matthew 25:14-30) to describe what is required of us when we enter our relationship with God through Him. We are born with natural abilities and are given specific spiritual gifts by the Holy Spirit as God's servants. God requires us to develop and use our natural abilities and to discover, develop and use our unique spiritual gifts to perform the good works He has prepared for us to perform. We will receive our reward when we obediently and faithfully develop and use our natural abilities and spiritual gifts to perform these good works. We will suffer loss when we fail to do this and lose the reward Jesus desires to give us. What we have received or acquired may be taken from us. Jesus stated relative to the reward He desires to give us in His final message in Revelation 22:12:

> "Behold, I am coming quickly, and My reward is with Me, to render to every man according to what he has done."

Jesus' reference to His reward can refer to the full reward we hope to receive as indicated by John in 2 John 1:8-9 and to the recompense we expect to receive for our deeds indicated by Paul in 2 Corinthians 5:10.

Jesus identified a fourth group in His parable of the talents who claim to be His followers during their lives. Some individuals in the first group mentioned earlier may be included in this group that will be judged with the unrighteous at the great white throne judgement. This group, represented by the slave with one talent who buried his talent, will have professed Jesus is Lord and indicated they believed God raised Him from the dead. However, there will be no evidence of His presence and the transforming influence of the Holy Spirit in their lives. Jesus will declare He never knew these individuals, and they will be judged and sentenced to the lake of fire.

The righteous who stand before Jesus who have faithfully demonstrated their love for, faith and trust in, and obedience to Him will enter the kingdom of heaven and be invited to enter the joy of their Lord. Their good works will be examined and judged by Jesus. Paul addressed this in 1 Corinthians 3:9-15. He stated:

> "For we are God's fellow workers; you are God's building. According to the grace of God which was given to me, like a wise master builder I laid a foundation, and another is building on it. But each man must be careful how he builds on it. For no man can lay a foundation other than the one which

is laid, which is Jesus Christ. Now if any man builds on the foundation with gold, silver, precious stones, wood, hay, straw, each man's work will become evident; for the day will show it because it is to be revealed with fire, and the fire itself will test the quality of each man's work. If any man's work is burned up, he will suffer loss; but he himself will be saved, yet so as through fire."

Jesus is the foundation on which we build our life and develop our character. We build on His foundation with care. The good works we do and our motives for doing them while building on Jesus' foundation will be revealed and tested with fire when we stand before Him. Good works represented by gold, silver and precious stones will be accepted by Jesus. Good works represented by wood, hay and straw will be rejected. We will receive a reward for those good works that are accepted, but we will suffer loss for those that are rejected. We will not lose our salvation because of those good works that are rejected. However, we may suffer loss with respect to our position in the kingdom of heaven. Our position will be fixed for eternity after our good works have been examined by Jesus; it will never change.

Summary

Questions are raised regarding those who have never had the opportunity to hear about God's saving grace through Jesus when His judgment is discussed. Paul responded to this in Romans 1:18-20 where he stated:

> "For the wrath of God is revealed from heaven against all ungodliness and unrighteousness of men who suppress the truth in unrighteousness, because that which is known about God is evident within them; for God made it evident to them. For since the creation of the world His invisible attributes, His eternal power and divine nature, have been clearly seen, being understood through what has been made, so that they are without excuse."

The existence of God has been made evident through His creation. He has placed a sense of "His invisible attributes, His eternal power and divine nature" within us "since the creation of the world." Therefore, the unrighteous who have rejected God will be without excuse when they stand before Jesus at the great white throne judgment.

Several observations can be made from the preceding discussions:

- There is a difference between the kingdom of God and the kingdom of heaven. We enter the kingdom of God when we receive Jesus as our Savior and Lord of our life. The righteous will enter the kingdom of heaven after their good works and their motives for performing them have been examined and judged by Jesus. Not everyone who believe they have entered the kingdom of God will enter the kingdom of heaven.

- We are to grow in our knowledge of and internalize God's word in the Bible when we enter a relationship with Him through Jesus. We are expected to obey Jesus' commandments and words and to perform the good works God has prepared for us to perform.

- Our faith in God and Jesus develops and grows, and They reveal Themselves to and take up residence in us with the Holy Spirit as we grow in our knowledge of and internalize God's word in the Bible, and we yield ourself in obedience to Them.

- Our love for Jesus and obedience to Him must be the foundation on which we build our life and develop our character. These must motivate the good works we perform in His name. We then join the ranks of the righteous, God blesses and rewards us, and our names are written in the book of life.

- Our faith atrophies and dies when we fail to grow in our knowledge of and internalize God's word in the Bible, build our life and develop our character on the foundation of Jesus, and yield ourself in faith and obedience to Jesus. God may withdraw His Spirit from us when these occurs, and we may join the ranks of the unrighteous.

- The righteous and unrighteous will be separated at the great white throne judgment. Everyone will be judged by the words Jesus spoke in the four Gospels. The unrighteous will then be judged by what is written about them in the books that will be opened at the great white thrown judgment and thrown into the lake of fire. Only the righteous whose names are written in the book of life will enter the kingdom of heaven.

- The good works of the righteous and their motives for doing them will be examined by Jesus. Some of their good works may be rejected, and they will suffer loss when this occurs. Other good works will be accepted, and they will receive a reward for them. This examination will determine the positions of the righteous in the kingdom of heaven for eternity.

- The righteous who have faithfully performed the "good works, which God prepared beforehand so that [they] would walk in them" will receive a reward when their good works are examined by Jesus.

- We do not know when Jesus will return or when we will breathe our last breath. We will spend eternity in the kingdom of heaven with God, Jesus, the Holy Spirit, the angels of God, and the righteous when we have had faith in, trusted and been obedient to Jesus during our life, and we have been fruitful in performing good works God has prepared for us to perform during our life. We will spend eternity in the lake of fire with Satan, his angels and the unrighteous when we have not sought and received God's redemption through Jesus. We will also be separated from God, Jesus and the Holy Spirit in the lake of fire when we have performed none of the good works God has prepared for us to perform in our relationship with Jesus during our life.

SHEOL, HADES, HELL, PARADISE AND HEAVEN

In Hebrews 9:27, the author stated:

> "And inasmuch as it is appointed for men to die once and after this comes judgement."

The Bible teaches our spirit and soul are separated from our physical body at the time of our death, and our physical body is placed in a grave in the ground. Sheol, Hades, hell, paradise and heaven refer to places where the Bible indicates our spirit and soul may go when we are judged by God after we die. Sheol is an Old Testament Hebrew word, and Hades is a New Testament Greek word that refer to the same place. Hell sometimes refers to the same place as Sheol and Hades in the Bible.

Jesus' parable of the rich man and Lazarus in Luke 16:16–31 presented a description of Hades/Sheol. They were a place that was divided into two regions. One region, referred to as Abraham's bosom, was a place of great comfort and rest. The righteous dead occupied this region. The other region, referred to as hell, was a place of great torment and suffering. The wicked dead occupied this region. A great chasm separated the two regions that prevented occupants of one region from crossing over to the other region.

Peter indicated in 1 Peter 3:18-20 Jesus went to Hades after He was "made alive in the spirit" after His crucifixion, but before the resurrection of His physical body where He made a "proclamation to the spirits now in prison" there. It is reasonable to presume these imprisoned spirits were in the region of Hades referred to as hell.

Jesus stated to the repentant criminal in Luke 23:43 while they hung on their crosses that he would be with Him that day in paradise. It is reasonable to presume Jesus went to Abraham's bosom in Hades where He made His proclamation to the spirits imprisoned in the region of Hades referred to as hell. Therefore, Jesus' reference to paradise may have referred to Abraham's bosom in Hades.

Matthew 27:52–53 implied the souls and spirits of the righteous in Abraham's bosom were released from Hades after Jesus' resurrection. They appeared to many in Jerusalem and then presumably were transported to heaven. Pauls' statement in Ephesians 4:8 implied this. Heaven at this time was and still is referred to as a spiritual realm.

Paul stated in 2 Corinthians 12:2–4 that he knew a man who 14 years earlier was caught up into the third heaven he referred to as paradise. This implied paradise is in heaven. This also implied Hades/Sheol only consisted of a single region where there is great torment and suffering, referred to as hell, after Jesus' resurrection.

Individuals when judged by God after they die will be received into heaven where there will be great comfort and rest when they have been redeemed by and reconciled to God through their faith and trust in and obedience to Jesus. They will be placed in hell when they have not sought and received God's redemption and reconciliation through Jesus where they will experience great torment and suffering.

THREE RESURRECTIONS

The Bible indicates there will be three resurrections where our spirits and souls will be reunited with physical bodies. They are:

- **The rapture** (Matthew 24:26-41, Mark 13:24-39 and Luke 17:22-37): The rapture will be a raising up of the living and a resurrection of the dead who have had faith in, trusted and were obedient to Jesus during their lives to meet Him in the air. Their names will be written in the book of life. The rapture will occur during the middle of the seven-year tribulation at the sounding of the 7th trumpet.

- **Resurrection of saints martyred during the great tribulation** (Revelation 20:4-6): This resurrection, referred to as the first resurrection in Revelation, will include those who remain faithful to God and Jesus and do not receive the mark of the beast during the great tribulation. Their names will be written in the book of life. This resurrection will occur after the return of Jesus at the end of the great tribulation and before He sets up His 1,000-year kingdom. Those in this resurrection will be priests of God and Jesus and will rule with Jesus during His 1,000-year kingdom.

- **Resurrection of the dead before the great white throne judgement at the end of Jesus' 1,000-year kingdom** (Revelation 20:11-15): This resurrection will include the dead who have not been redeemed by and reconciled to God through Jesus before the rapture and who have received the mark of the beast during the great tribulation. Their names will not be written in the book of life. This resurrection will also include all who die during Jesus' 1,000-year kingdom and who die at the end of His 1,000-year kingdom when the first earth and heaven pass away. Some will have been faithful and obedient to Jesus, and their names will be written in the book of life. Others will have rejected Jesus, and their names will not be written in the book of life. This last resurrection occurs after the first earth and heaven pass away at the end of Jesus' 1,000-year kingdom and before the great white throne judgement.

The names of those in the rapture, the first resurrection, and who are faithful to and obey Jesus during His 1,000-year kingdom will be written in the book of life. They will be immortal after their resurrections. Those in the resurrection before the great white throne judgement whose names are not written in the book of life will be placed in the lake of fire where they will be tormented and suffer forever.

OUR REWARD IN THE KINGDOM OF HEAVEN

Isaiah stated in Isaiah 40:10:

> "Behold, the LORD God will come with might,
> With His arm ruling for Him.
> Behold, His reward is with Him
> And His recompense before Him."

Jesus stated in Revelation 22:12:

> "Behold, I am coming quickly, and My reward is with Me, to render to every
> man according to what he has done."

Jesus will fulfill Isaiah's prophesy when He returns.

The Bible teaches we are to study and internalize God's word in the Bible. We will spiritually grow and mature through this study as our mind is renewed and our heart is transformed through the actions of the Holy Spirit in our life. As we spiritually grow and mature, we are to develop our natural abilities, discover and develop our spiritual gifts, and employ them in doing good works the Holy Spirit calls us to enter and perform.

John encouraged us in 2 John 1:8-9 to abide in the teachings of Jesus so that we will receive a full reward. Paul stated in 2 Corinthians 5:10 we will stand before the judgement seat of Jesus so that we can be recompensed for our deeds in the body. Paul indicated in 1 Corinthians 3:12-15 the quality of our works will be revealed and tested by fire when we stand before Jesus on the last day. Some works will be burned up while others will remain. We will suffer loss for our works that are burned up, but we will not lose our salvation through Jesus. Jesus, John and Paul indicated the righteous will receive a reward for the good works they have done when Jesus returns. However, they do not present information as to what this reward will be.

Jesus provided clues in His discourses in Matthew 24:42-51 and Matthew 25:14-36 regarding this reward. The faithful and sensible slave in Matthew 24:42-51 was put in charge of all his master's possessions. The slaves who were given two and five talents in Matthew 25:14-36 were told they will be put in charge of many things because of their faithfulness over a few things. These two discourses imply the reward the righteous will receive from Jesus will be related to positions of responsibility and leadership they will be given in the kingdom of heaven. These positions when awarded will be fixed for eternity.

Paul described three crowns in his letters the righteous will receive as a reward in the kingdom of heaven. They are:

The Crown of Righteousness: The crown of righteousness will be given to all those who have loved Jesus' appearing (2 Timothy 4:7-8).

The Crown of Life: The crown of life will be given to those who have persevered under trials (James 1:12, Revelation 2:10).

The Crown of Glory: The crown of glory will be given to elders (pastors) who have been faithful in shepherding the flocks (churches) that have been entrusted to their care (1 Peter 5:1-4).

The Imperishable Crown: The imperishable crown will be given to those who discipline their bodies to bring it into subjection to the righteousness of God. (1 Corinthians 9:25)

The Crown of Rejoicing: The crown of rejoicing will be given to those who rejoice at the coming of Jesus (1 Thessalonians 2:19).

THE NATURE OF OUR RESURRECTED BODIES

Paul gave us insight into the nature of the resurrection bodies the righteous will receive in 1 Corinthians 15:35-49. He stated:

> "But someone will say, 'How are the dead raised? And with what kind of body do they come?' You fool! That which you sow does not come to life unless it dies; and that which you sow, you do not sow the body which is to be, but a bare grain, perhaps of wheat or of something else. But God gives it a body just as He wished, and to each of the seeds a body of its own.

All flesh is not the same flesh, but there is one flesh of men, and another flesh of beasts, and another flesh of birds, and another of fish. There are also heavenly bodies and earthly bodies, but the glory of the heavenly is one, and the glory of the earthly is another. There is one glory of the sun, and another glory of the moon, and another glory of the stars; for star differs from star in glory. So also is the resurrection of the dead. It is sown a perishable body, it is raised an imperishable body; it is sown in dishonor, it is raised in glory; it is sown in weakness, it is raised in power; it is sown a natural body, it is raised a spiritual body. If there is a natural body, there is also a spiritual body. So also it is written, 'The first man, Adam, became a living soul.' Genesis 2:7 The last Adam became a life-giving spirit. However, the spiritual is not first, but the natural; then the spiritual. The first man is from the earth, earthy; the second man is from heaven. As is the earthy, so also are those who are earthy; and as is the heavenly, so also are those who are heavenly. Just as we have borne the image of the earthy, we will also bear the image of the heavenly."

The natural bodies of the righteous are perishable, weak and given to dishonor because of sin. Their resurrection bodies, however, will be bodies that will be raised imperishable in power and glory. The man from heaven is Jesus. The resurrection bodies of the righteous will be bodies that will be like Jesus' resurrection body. Paul affirmed this in Philippians 3:20-21:

"For our citizenship is in heaven, from which also we eagerly wait for a Savior, the Lord Jesus Christ; who will transform the body of our humble state into conformity with the body of His glory, by the exertion of the power that He has even to subject all things to Himself."

John reaffirmed this in 1 John 3:1-2:

"See how great a love the Father has bestowed on us, that we would be called children of God; and such we are. For this reason the world does not know us, because it did not know Him. Beloved, now we are children of God, and it has not appeared as yet what we will be. We know that when He appears, we will be like Him, because we will see Him just as He is."

The bodies of the righteous, like Jesus, will be placed in a grave when they die. Their bodies when resurrected will be like Jesus' resurrected body. They will:

- Consist of flesh and bones (Luke 24:39-40),
- Be similar in appearance to their natural bodies (Matthew 28:8-10, Luke 24:13-35, John 20:11-18),
- Be able to eat food (Luke 24:41-43, John 21:12-13),
- Be able to appear and disappear at will (Mark 16:12-14, Luke 24:31, 36-37, John 20:19-20, 26), and
- Be imperishable, eternal and immortal (1 Corinthians 15:53-54, 2 Corinthians 5:1).

Jesus stated in Matthew 22:30 and Luke 20:36 that we will be like angels with our resurrection bodies. The resurrection bodies of the righteous will not be corrupted by sin nor be subject to the constraints of known laws of physics and time even though they may resemble their natural bodies.

THE BOOK OF LIFE

Exodus 32:33 is the first reference to God's book in the Bible. The LORD said to Moses in response to the Israelites building and worshiping a golden calf after Moses had led them out of Egypt, "Whoever has sinned against Me, I will blot him out of My book." Other references to God's book in the Old Testament include:

- The Psalmist petitioned the LORD in Psalms 69:28 regarding those who were persecuting and afflicting him. He wrote, "May they be blotted out of the book of life and may they not be recorded with the righteous.
- The Psalmist wrote in Psalms 139:16, "Your eyes have seen my unformed substance; and in Your book were all written the days that were ordered for me, when as yet there was not one of them."
- The angel Gabriel told Daniel in Daniel 12:1:

  "Now at that time Michael, the great prince who stands guard over the sons of your people, will arise and there will be a time of distress such as never occurred since there was a nation until that time; and at that time your people, everyone who is found written in the book, will be rescued."

The names written in *My book* in Exodus 33:32, the *book of life* in Psalms 69:28, *Your book* in Psalms 139:16, and the *book* in Daniel 12:1 in the Old Testament referred to names written in *God's book*. The names written in the *book of life* mentioned in Philippians 4:3 and Revelation 3:5 and 21:27 in the New Testament can also refer to names written ins *God's book*.

God stated He will remove our name from His book when we have sinned against Him. The Bible teaches this will occur unless we repent of our sins and receive the redemption and reconciliation God extends to us through the blood of Jesus. We enter a reconciled relationship with God through Jesus when we approach Him, repent of our sins, and receive His gift of grace. We then begin a process through which God's book becomes for us the book of life. This process is discussed in Chapter 4. John was told in Revelation 20:15:

> "And if anyone's name was not found written in the book of life, he was thrown into the lake of fire."

Jesus stated in Revelations 3:5:

> "He who overcomes will thus be clothed in white garments; and I will not erase his name from the book of life, and I will confess his name before My Father and before His angels."

Jesus' statement is a conditional statement. Our name will not be removed from the book of life when we have overcome temptation. The Bible implies this occurs when we overcome the trials and tribulations associated with our relationship with God through Jesus, and we have demonstrated our faith and trust in and our obedience to Jesus' words in this relationship. Jesus' statement also implies our name may be removed from the book of life when we have not overcome these trials and tribulations nor remained faithful and obedient to Jesus' words.

The Bible does not indicate during our life when God may remove our name from His book. The Bible also does not indicate when our name transitions from being written in God's book to being written in the book of life after we have entered a relationship with Him through Jesus.

Peter stated in 2 Peter 3:9:

> "The Lord is not slow about His promise, as some count slowness, but is patient toward you, not wishing for any to perish but for all to come to repentance."

Paul stated in 1 Timothy 2:4 that God "desires all men to be saved and to come to the knowledge of the truth." God does not desire anyone's name to be removed from His book. Therefore, the Holy Spirit acts throughout our life to convict us of sin and draw us to repent and enter a reconciled relationship with God through Jesus. How we choose to respond to these acts of the Holy Spirit is up to us. Some choose to reject God, Jesus and the Holy

Spirit. Some choose to enter a relationship with God through Jesus at an early age. Others make this choice later in their life. Some make this choice at the time of their death. God honors all these responses. However, He will remove our name from His book when our response has been to reject Him, Jesus and the Holy Spirit.

Psalms 139:16 indicates God has written our name in His book before we are born. Peter and Paul stated God desires "for all to come to repentance" and "to be saved and to come to the knowledge of the truth." The Bible teaches God through His grace provides the means through which we can be redeemed and reconciled to Him through our faith and trust in and obedience to Jesus. The Holy Spirit convicts us of sin and draws us to repent and enter a relationship with God through Jesus. We then begin a process through which our name will transition from being written in God's book to being written in the book of life. This occurs as we grow in our knowledge of and internalize God's word in the Bible, and we enter and perform the good works He prepares for us. Jesus' statement indicated He will not remove our name from the book of life when we persevere and overcome the trials and tribulations we encounter because of our relationship with Him.

The Bible implies God will remove from His book the names of those who:

- Have sinned against Him (Exodus 33:32) and have not repented and received the redemption He extends to them through the blood of Jesus;

- Go on "sinning willfully after receiving the knowledge of the truth" (Hebrews 10:26-31);

- "After they have escaped the defilement of the world by the knowledge of the Lord and Savior Jesus Christ, they are again entangled in them and are overcome" by them (2 Peter 2:20-21);

- "Have once been enlightened and have tasted of the heavenly gift and have been made partakers of the Holy Spirit, and have tasted the good word of God and the power of the ages to come, and then have fallen away" from Him, Jesus and the Holy Spirit (Hebrews 6:4-6);

- Have only ministered to others in the name of Jesus to achieve personal gain and be noticed by others (Matthew 6:1-7, 25:31-46);

- Have done nothing to spiritually grow and mature in their relationship with Jesus after entering this relationship and have performed none of the good works God has prepared for them to perform (Matthew 25:14-30, Luke 19:12-27, and John 15:1-3); and

- Will worship the Antichrist during the great tribulation (Revelation 13:8, 17:8).

The Bible does not indicate when during the life of an individual his name may be removed from God's book. However, in Hebrews 9:27, the author indicated when this may occur:

"And inasmuch as it is appointed for men to die once and after this comes judgment, so Christ also, having been offered once to bear the sins of many, will appear a second time for salvation without reference to sin, to those who eagerly await Him."

We will be judged by God after we die. Our position with Him will be fixed at this judgment for eternity. The names of those mentioned in the Bible verses listed in the preceding paragraph will have been removed from God's book when they stand before Jesus at the great white throne judgment. They will be thrown into the lake of fire because their names will not be written in the book of life.

God knows we will experience temptations and encounter challenges, adversities and persecution when we honor and obey Jesus' words. He knows we will not live a sinless life after we enter a reconciled relationship with Him through Jesus. He knows we will sometimes fail to obey Jesus' words and do some of the good works He has prepared for us. However, God through His grace extended to us through the atoning blood of Jesus will forgive us when these occur, and we seek His forgiveness. God is glorified by our perseverance demonstrated through performing the good works He has prepared for us (Matthew 5:16). Our names as a result will be written in the book of life.

The names of those who have not been removed from God's book will be written in the book of life. These individuals will stand before Jesus at a separate judgment on the last day (2 Corinthians 5:10). Some of their works may be rejected while others will be accepted when Jesus examines their life (1 Corinthians 3:9-15). They will receive their reward (Jeremiah 17:10, 1 John 1:8, Revelation 22:12) given to them by Jesus and enter the kingdom of heaven.

THE LAKE OF FIRE - THE SECOND DEATH

The lake of fire is referred to as the place of the second death in Revelation 20:14 and 21:18. The term second death refers to eternal separation from God, Jesus and the Holy Spirit. Jesus stated in Matthew 25:41 the unrighteous will be sent to "the eternal fire prepared for the devil and his angels." The lake of fire will be populated by:

- Satan (Revelation 20:10),
- The fallen angels (or demons) (2 Peter 2:4, Jude 6-7),
- The Antichrist and false prophet (Revelation 19:20),
- Death and Hades (Revelation 20:13), and
- Unrighteous whose names are not written in the book of life (Revelation 20:15).

Jesus indicated the lake of fire will be a place of:

- Unquenchable fire (Matthew 3:12),
- Unbearable thirst (Luke 16:24),
- Darkness (Matthew 25:30),
- Weeping and gnashing of teeth (Matthew 24:15, 25:30),
- Memory and remorse (Luke 16:19-31),
- Eternal fire (Matthew 25:41), and
- Eternal punishment (Matthew 25:46).

There is symbolism and reality in the Bible's description of the lake of fire. Fire symbolizes judgment and separation. The lake of fire will be a physical place. It will be a place of eternal punishment and separation from God, Jesus and the Holy Spirit. God will place an eternal barrier between those who will be with Him, Jesus and the Holy Spirit throughout eternity and those who will be eternally separated from Them.

Jesus referred to the lake of fire as a place of darkness. The darkness will be real darkness. It will also be a darkness associated with the absence of God. There will be no righteousness when God is absent; there will only be evil. There is no truth; there is only deception and despair. All that gives worth, value and meaning to life is stripped away when God is absent. This is the darkness that will exist in the lake of fire.

We often only consider God's attributes of love, mercy and grace; we ignore His attributes of holiness and justice. These attributes require God to judge the conscious and deliberate choices the unrighteous make during their lives to disobey His commandments and laws and to reject, revile and dishonor Him. God would diminish Himself if He did not act justly toward those who blatantly defied Him. Therefore, the lake of fire will be a place of God's eternal justice.

The unrighteous will suffer greatly in the lake of fire. It will be a place of great physical suffering. The unrighteous will have memory; they will know why they are there and what they are missing by being eternally separated from God. The emotional responses of shame, anguish, regret and remorse will torment them forever.

John was told in Revelation the unrighteous who worship the Antichrist and receive his mark (the mark of the beast) during the great tribulation will:

- Experience the undiluted divine wrath of God (Revelation 14:9-10),
- Have no rest both day and night (Revelation 14:11), and
- Be tormented both day and night forever (Revelation 14:11, 20:10).

CHAPTER 8
CREATION OF A NEW HEAVEN, EARTH AND JERUSALEM

DESTRUCTION OF THE FIRST HEAVEN AND FIRST EARTH

Revelation 20:11 indicates earth and heaven will flee from Him who sits on the great white throne. Revelation 21:1 states the first heaven and earth will pass away. There is no other mention in Revelation regarding the destruction of the earth and heaven. However, Peter presented an image of the destruction of the heavens and earth in 2 Peter 3:10:12:

> "But the day of the Lord will come like a thief, in which the heavens will pass away with a roar and the elements will be destroyed with intense heat, and the earth and its works will be burned up."

SIGNIFICANCE OF ZION

Jesus stated to His disciples in John 14:1-4:

> "Do not let your heart be troubled; believe in God, believe also in Me. In My Father's house are many dwelling places; if it were not so, I would have told you so; for I go to prepare a place for you. If I go and prepare a place for you, I will come again and receive you to Myself, that where I am, there you may be also. And you know the way where I am going."

Jesus indicated there are many dwelling places in His Father's house. The Psalms and Hebrews appear to present information on the location and description of this house. Psalms 9:11 states:

> "Sing praises to the LORD, who dwells in Zion,
> Declare among the peoples His deeds."

and Psalms 132:13-14 state:

"For the LORD has chosen Zion;
He has desired it for His habilitation.
'This is My resting place forever;
Here I will dwell, for I have desired it.'"

Psalms 48:1-3, 8, 12-14 present a description of Zion's beauty:

"Great is the LORD, and greatly to be praised,
In the city of our God, His holy mountain.
Beautiful in elevation, the joy of the whole earth,
Is Mount Zion in the far north,
The city of the great King. God, in her palaces,
Has made Himself known as a stronghold."
...
"As we have heard, so have we seen
In the city of the LORD of hosts, in the city of our God,
God will establish her forever. Selah."
...
"Walk about Zion and go around her;
Count her towers;
Consider her ramparts;
Go through her palaces,
That you may tell it to the next generation.
For such is God,
Our God forever and ever;
He will guide us until death."

Another description of Zion is found in Hebrews 12:22-24:

"But you have come to Mount Zion and to the city of the living God, the heavenly Jerusalem, and to myriads of angels, to the general assembly and church of the firstborn who are enrolled in heaven, and to God, the Judge of all, and to the spirits of the righteous made perfect, and to Jesus, the mediator of a new covenant, and to the sprinkled blood, which speaks better than the blood of Abel."

Readers of the Old Testament often believed *Zion* is a Hebrew word that came into use as a religious term long after Jerusalem became a city. *Zion* historically predated the

Israelites and initially had no association with religious beliefs. The word *Zion* has an Arabic origin. The root Hebrew word for *Zion* means *dry place* or *parched ground*. Whereas the Arabic root word for *Zion* more appropriately means *hill crest* or *mountainous ridge*. The knoll or rounded hilltop of the ancient village of Jerusalem was called Zion before Jerusalem became a village.

Zion was first mentioned in 2 Samuel 5:7. It was located on the easternmost knoll of the two knolls that encompassed the ancient village of Jerusalem (Figure 8). Zion initially referred to the Jebusite fortress that was conquered by David. The area of and around the fort00ress became known as the City of David after being conquered by David.

Mount Zion initially referred to the location of the Jebusite fortress. The location of Mount Zion was moved to the top of the eastern Jerusalem knoll after the Temple of Solomon (the first Jewish temple) was erected there. This location is called the Temple Mount today. The final and current location of Mount Zion was moved to the more prominent western Jerusalem knoll. This is believed to be the location of the palace of king David. This location is west of the location of the City of David across the Tyropoeon Valley that separates the two knolls.

Zion has many meanings in ancient and modern Israel and in Old and New Testament history. It refers to the City of David, the ancient and modern City of Jerusalem, and the nation of Israel. With respect to Old and New Testament history, Zion is identified as the city of our God, the city of the LORD of hosts, the city of the living God, My holy mountain, etc. Zion along with Mount Zion represented the places throughout Old and New Testament history where God was believed to be present. Zion is the thread that ties together many of the narratives associated with Old Testament historic events. These events ultimately will lead to the future new Jerusalem, which God is building and will come down from heaven after heaven and earth pass away. "The Lord God the Almighty and the Lamb (Jesus)" will be its temple, and they will dwell there forever with the Holy Spirit, myriads of angels, and the righteous whose names are written in the Lamb's book of life. The new Jerusalem will be the house Jesus referred to in John 14:1-4 that His Father is building with many dwelling places for the righteous who will enter the kingdom of heaven.

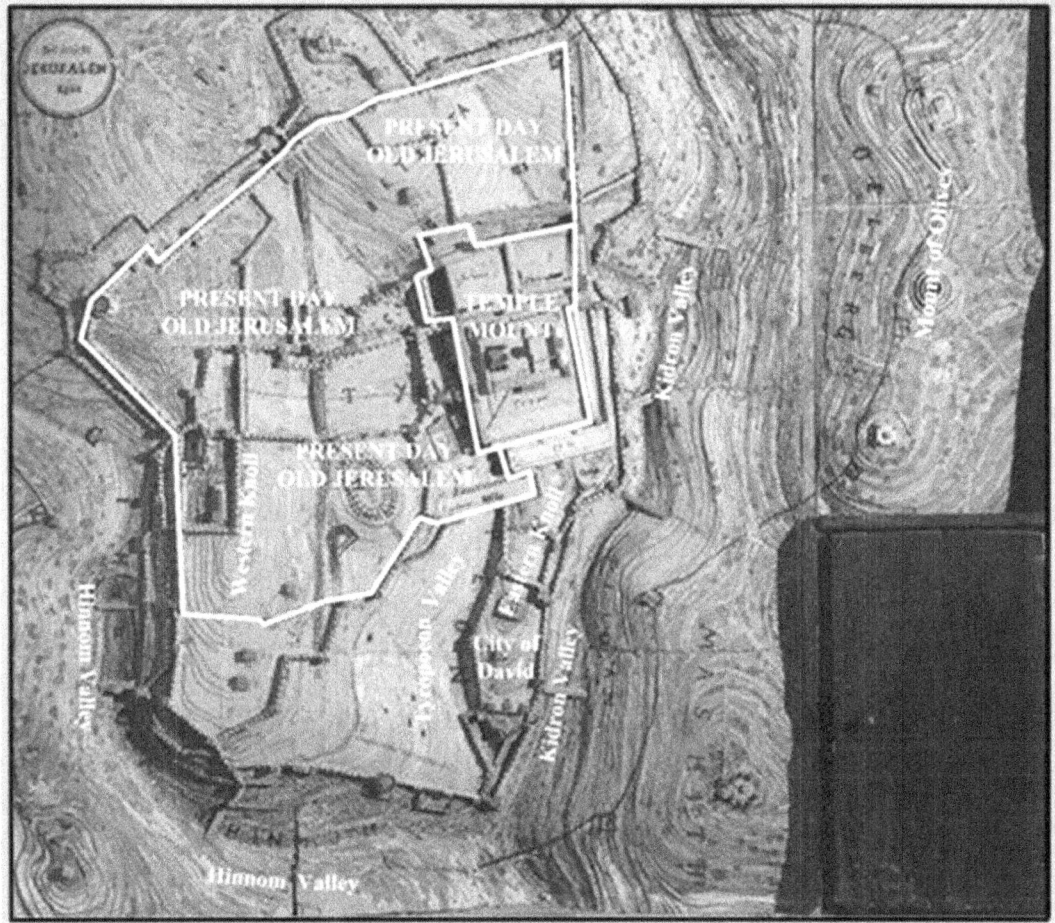

Thee Dimensional Model of Jerusalem: Conrad S. Schick (1822-1901) was a famous architect who lived in Jerusalem at the end of the 19th century. He created the three dimensional model as he envisioned Jerusalem during the Second Temple period shown in the above image. The size of this model was 99 by 85 cm, and its scale was 1:2500.

(Image photo contours sharpened and labeling and drawing of present day old Jerusalem boundaries added by D. D. Reynolds)

(Original Image sources: http://www.templemount.org/topo.html)

Figure 8

THE NEW EARTH, HEAVEN AND JERUSALEM

John was given a vision of the new heaven, earth and Jerusalem after his vision of the great white throne judgment in Revelation 21:1-3. The first heaven and earth had passed away. This is a confirmation of God's promised in Isaiah 65:17:

> "For behold, I create new heavens and a new earth;
> And the former things will not be remembered or come to mind."

His reference to new heavens refers to heavens that will exist beyond the new earth. These can refer to the creation of new or the recreation of existing solar systems and galaxies that will exist in the new heavens beyond the new earth. Regarding this promise, John "heard a loud voice from the throne saying (Revelation 21:3-7)":

> "'Behold, the tabernacle of God is among men, and He will dwell among them, and they shall be His people, and God Himself will be among them, and He will wipe away every tear from their eyes; and there will no longer be any death; there will no longer be any mourning, or crying, or pain; the first things have passed away.' And He who sits on the throne said, 'Behold, I am making all things new.' And He said, 'Write, for these words are faithful and true.' Then He said to me, 'It is done. I am the Alpha and the Omega, the beginning and the end. I will give to the one who thirsts from the spring of the water of life without cost. He who overcomes will inherit these things, and I will be His God and he will be My son.'"

This verse and Isaiah 65:17 indicate God will create a new earth and heaven and a new solar system and galaxies that will exist in the heavens beyond the new earth.

Heaven and earth are currently separated by sin. There will be no sin on the new earth and in the new heaven God will create. Therefore, Revelation 21:3-7 indicates the new heaven will be on the new earth because God will be there. Jesus stated in Mathew 22:30 we will have bodies in heaven like angels. **Therefore, our bodies on the new earth will be immortal, and we will live there with God forever.**

John was also told the new heaven and earth will have no more:

- Hunger, thirst and heat from the sun (Revelation 7:16),
- Tears, death, mourning, crying and pain (Revelation 21:4),
- Sin (Revelation 21:27), and
- Curse (Revelation 22:3).

Our spirit and soul enter the current heaven when we die. This will be a transitional heaven. Our body there will be a spiritual body with a recognizable form and characteristics but with no mass. We will reside in this heaven from the time we die until we are resurrected at the rapture or at the great white throne judgement.

Our spiritual body receives physical mass in the resurrection process when we are resurrected at the rapture or at the great white thrown judgement. We will have an immortal physical body when we enter the new heaven on the new earth.

Jesus gave us an understanding of the significance of the kingdom of heaven in Matthew 13:44-50 as it relates to our position in the new heaven on a new earth. He indicated the kingdom of heaven will be like:

- A treasure hidden in a field that, when found, the finder sells everything he has so he can buy the field because of his great joy over finding it.

- A merchant who seeks fine pearls. When he finds one of great value, he sells everything he has so he can buy it.

- A dragnet that is cast into the sea to gather every kind of fish. It is dragged to the beach when it is filled where the good fish are separated from the bad. The good fish are placed in containers, and the bad are thrown away.

Jesus then stated in Mathew 13:49-50:

> "So it will be at the end of ages; the angels shall come forth, and take out the wicked from among the righteous, and they will throw them into the furnace of fire; in that place there will be weeping and gnashing of teeth."

John was given a vision associated with this separating in Revelation 14:14-20.

Jesus taught two important principles with respect to the new heaven and earth in the above verses in Matthew. First, the value of our ability to enter and live in the new heaven on the new earth is priceless; we would sell everything we own to purchase our entrance if we could. However, the Bible teaches it is impossible for us to enter the kingdom of heaven, relying on our own merit or worth. The Bible further teaches Jesus has paid the admission price for us. Second, the righteous and unrighteous will be separated at the end of the ages. The righteous, who have loved Jesus and obeyed the words He spoke, will reside in the new heaven, earth and Jerusalem. The unrighteous who have rejected Jesus will be thrown into the lake of fire.

John received a vision of the new Jerusalem in Revelation 21:10-25. The new Jerusalem in this vision appeared to descend from God from the existing heaven where it was created.

It was suspended in midair above the new earth and showed the glory of God. John's vision indicated the new Jerusalem will:

- Be laid out in the shape of a cube (Revelation 21:16). Its length, width and height will each be 1,500 miles (2,414 kilometers). This is equal to the distance East-to-West from New York City to Denver, Colorado, and North-to-South from Canada to Florida in the United States.

- Have twelve gates (Revelation 21:12-13). There will be three gates each on the east, north, south and west sides of the city. An angel who will have one of the names of the twelve tribes of Israel written on him will be at each gate. Each gate will be made from a single pearl.

- Be separated into twelve levels (Revelation 21:14, 18-20). The city will be pure gold like clear glass, and the foundation stone of each level will be a different precious gem. The gems will be jasper, sapphire, chalcedony, emerald, sardonyx, sardius, chrysolite, beryl, topaz, chrysoprase, jacinth and amethyst. Each level will carry the name of one of the twelve apostles of Jesus. The walls of each level will be 216 feet (65.8 meters) high and made of jasper.

- Have streets made of pure gold (Revelation 21:21). The gold will be like transparent glass.

- Have no temple (Revelation 21:22). God and Jesus will be its temple.

- Have no need for the sun or moon (Revelation 21:23). The glory of God will illuminate the city, and its lamp will be Jesus.

- Have a river of the water of life flowing from the throne of God and Jesus (Revelation 22:1-2).

The water will be clear as crystal. On each side of the river will be the tree of life, which will bear twelve kinds of fruit and yield its fruit every month. Its leaves will be for the healing of the nations.

Adam and Eve were driven from the Garden of Eden after they had sinned to prevent them from eating the fruit from the tree of life and live forever in a sinful state eternally separated from God (Genesis 3:22-23). This would have separated them and all men and women from God forever. The tree of life was then removed from the earth. It will, however, grow in the new Jerusalem, and its fruit will be available as food for the inhabitants of the city.

God initiated a system of offerings and feasts the Israelites were to offer and celebrate to temporarily atone for their sins and maintain fellowship with Him. These all pointed to the ultimate sacrifice Jesus was to make of Himself on a cross to atone for our sins.

The offerings and two of the seven feasts initiated by God will be celebrated as a memorial to and in remembrance of what Jesus accomplished on the cross during the 1,000-year kingdom of Jesus. There will be no sin in the new earth, heaven and Jerusalem. Therefore, there will be no offerings and feasts to atone for sin in the new earth, heaven and Jerusalem.

The new Jerusalem will be the dwelling place of the heavenly hosts and saints of God. This will include God the Father and Jesus (Revelation 21:22, 22:1), the Holy Spirit (Revelation 22:17), and the myriads of angels who faithfully serve God (Hebrews 12:22-24). The angel in Revelation 21:9 referred to the new Jerusalem as the wife of the Lamb, implying the new Jerusalem will be the final dwelling place of the body of Christ, the Church. It will be the place Jesus' Father has prepared for men and women throughout the ages who trusted and had faith in His Son and who were obedient to Him. The angel told John in Revelation 21:27 only persons whose names are written in the Lamb's book of life will be allowed to enter the new Jerusalem.

John stated in Revelation 21:22-27:

> "I saw no temple in [the new Jerusalem], for the Lord God the Almighty and the Lamb are its temple. And the city has no need of the sun or of the moon to shine on it, for the glory of God has illumined it, and its lamp is the Lamb. The nations will walk by its light, and the kings of the earth will bring their glory into it. In the daytime (for there will be no night there) its gates will never be closed; and they will bring the glory and the honor of the nations into it; and nothing unclean, and no one who practices abomination and lying, shall ever come into it, but only those whose names are written in the Lamb's book of life."

The above vision affirms the Lord's intention to repopulate the new earth He indicated He will create in Isaiah 65:17.

The Lord then continued in Isaiah 65:18-23:

> "But be glad and rejoice forever in what I create;
> For behold, I create Jerusalem for rejoicing
> And her people for gladness.
> And there will no longer be heard in her
> The voice of weeping and the sound of crying.
> No longer will there be in it an infant who lives but a few days,
> Or an old man who does not live out his days;
> For the youth will die at the age of one hundred
> And the one who does not reach the age of one hundred
> Will be thought accursed.

They will build houses and inhabit them;
They will also plant vineyards and eat their fruit.
They will not build and another inhabit,
They will not plant and another eat;
For as the lifetime of a tree, so will be the days of My people,
And My chosen ones will wear out the work of their hands.
They will not labor in vain,
Or bear children for calamity;
For they are the offspring of those blessed by the LORD,
And their descendants with them."

The LORD concluded in Isaiah 66:22-24:

"'For just as the new heavens and the new earth
Which I make will endure before Me,' declares the LORD,
'So your offspring and your name will endure.
And it shall be from new moon to new moon
And from Sabbath to Sabbath,
All mankind will come to bow down before
Me,' says the LORD.
'Then they will go forth and look
On the corpses of the men
Who have transgressed against Me.
For their worm will not die
And their fire will not be quenched;
And they will be an abhorrence to all mankind.'"

The following observations can be made from the above scripture verses and preceding discussions:

- The righteous whose names are written in the Lamb's book of life will live forever in the new Jerusalem. They will be immortal with bodies like angels (Mathew 22:30). Their positions in the new heaven and earth will be determined by the results of their examination by Jesus and the reward they will receive from Him. This position will be fixed forever. They will neither marry nor conceive children.

- Individuals who repopulate the new earth will have long lifespans. They will be mortal and eventually die. They will marry, conceive and give birth to children.

- The kings of the new earth will bring the glory and honor of the nations into the new Jerusalem, and nations will come to bow down before the LORD.
- The bodies of the unrighteous who have been condemned to the lake of fire will be observable and looked on by the inhabitants of the new earth as an example of those who have transgressed against God.

Finally, John stated in Revelation 22:1-5:

> "Then [the angel] showed me a river of the water of life, clear as crystal, coming from the Throne of God and of the Lamb, in the middle of its street. On either side of the river was the tree of life, bearing twelve kinds of fruit, yielding its fruit every month; and the leaves of the tree were for the healing of the nations. There will no longer be any curse; and the throne of God and of the Lamb will be in it, and His bondservants will serve Him; they will see His face, and His name will be on their foreheads. And there will no longer be any night; and they will not have need of the light of a lamp nor the light of the sun, because the Lord God will illumine them; and they will reign forever and ever."

The righteous, whose names are written in the Lamb's book of life, will see the face of Jesus in the new Jerusalem. His name will be written on their foreheads, and they will serve and reign with Him forever.

CHAPTER 9
JESUS - OUR HOPE FOR THE FUTURE

THE SECURITY OF GOD AND SUPREMACY OF JESUS

We are secure in our relationship with God through our faith and trust in and obedience to Jesus. Nothing can separate us from God and Jesus in this relationship. Jesus stated in John 10:27-30:

> "My sheep hear My voice, and I know them, and they follow Me; and I give eternal life to them, and they will never perish; and no one will snatch them out of My hand. My Father, who has given them to Me, is greater than all; and no one is able to snatch them out of the Father's hand. I and the Father are one."

Paul described the relationship we have with God through Jesus in Romans 8:15-17:

> "For you have not received a spirit of slavery leading to fear again, but you have received a spirit of adoption as sons by which we cry out, 'Abba! Father!' The Spirit Himself testifies with our spirit that we are children of God, and if children, heirs also, heirs of God and fellow heirs with Christ, if indeed we suffer with Him so we may also be glorified with Him."

We become adopted children of God through our relationship with Jesus and joint heirs with Jesus of God with all the privileges of being an heir of God.

Paul implied our relationship with Jesus will result in difficult life challenges and suffering. Jesus affirmed in Matthew 28:19, "All authority has been given to Me in heaven and on earth." He has authority in our relationship with Him to equip us through the presence of the Holy Spirit in our life with the means to persevere through and triumph over difficult life challenges and suffering in our life that may appear to overwhelm us.

THE PROMISES OF JESUS IN REVELATION 2 AND 3

God's righteousness and justice will ultimately prevail in the conflict between good and evil. He instructed us to have faith and trust Him in difficult and troubled times. David stated in Psalm 37:38-40:

> "But transgressors will be altogether destroyed; the posterity of the wicked will be cut off. But the salvation of the righteous is from the LORD; He is their strength in time of trouble. And the LORD helps them, and delivers them; He delivers them from the wicked, and saves them, because they take refuge in Him."

Jesus delivered messages to seven churches in Asia in Chapters 2 and 3 of Revelation. These were actual churches during John's day. Some Bible scholars today indicate these churches represented churches with different cultural, sociological and theological characteristics that have existed down through the ages and that exist today. Others indicate they represented different church ages from the days of the apostles to the present day.

Jesus' promises at the end of each message can be interpreted to be specific to the people of each church or church age. He prefaced each promise with the statement, "He who has an ear, let him hear what the Spirit says to the churches." The promises were made to those who would remain faithful and obedient to Him in each church or church age. We can argue that all seven promises apply equally to all who have been and will remain faithful and obedient to Jesus throughout the ages.

Jesus prefaced each promise with the phrase, "to him who overcomes." He will grant what He has promised to those who persevere through difficult times, hardships and trials that result from their faith and trust in and obedience to Him. Jesus promised those who overcomes:

Promise 1:

> "To him who overcomes, I will grant to eat of the tree of life, which is in the paradise of God." (Revelation 2:7)

Adam and Eve were driven from the garden of Eden when they disobeyed God and sinned, so they would not be able to eat the fruit of the tree of life and be eternally separated from God (Genesis 3:22-24). The tree of life then disappeared from the earth. The tree of life will be present in the new Jerusalem, and all whose names are written in the book of life will be allowed to eat its fruit. Access to the tree of life was the first thing that was denied Adam and Eve after they had sinned; it is the first thing Jesus promised to return to the righteous in His eternal kingdom.

Promise 2:

"He who overcomes will not be hurt by the second death." (Revelation 2:11)

All whose names are written in the book of life will not experience the second death that is eternal separation from God.

Promise 3:

"To him who overcomes, to him I will give some of the hidden manna, and I will give him a white stone, and a new name written on the stone which no one knows but he who receives it." (Revelation 2:17)

The manna that was given to the Israelites during their forty-year journey in the wilderness was enough to satisfy the needs of their physical hunger (Exodus 16:3-18). The hidden manna can refer to the sufficiency of God's grace that is extended to the righteous through Jesus to satisfy their spiritual hunger (John 6:47-51). A white stone during John's day was used to vote for the acquittal of an accused person. This statement indicates the righteous will be acquitted before God and given new names in His eternal kingdom.

Promise 4:

"And he who overcomes, and he who keeps My deeds until the end, to him I will give authority over the nations; and he shall rule them with a rod of iron, as the vessels of the potter are broken to pieces, as I also have received authority from my Father; and I will give him the morning star." (Revelation 2:26-28)

This is the only one of Jesus' seven promises with a condition in addition to remaining faithful and obedient to Him. This condition is a possible reference to Jesus' statement in His parable of the talents (Matthew 25:14- 30). He indicated those who are faithful to perform the good works God prepares for them during their lives will be given the authority to exercise leadership in His eternal kingdom. Lucifer was called the star of the morning in Isaiah 14:12 before he rebelled and sinned against God. This was a reference to the special position he had in God's kingdom before he was cast out of heaven. To be given the morning star can imply those who meet the special condition of this promise will be given special positions in God's eternal kingdom.

Promise 5:

> "He who overcomes will be thus clothed in white garments; and I will not erase his name from the book of life, and I will confess his name before My Father and before His angels." (Revelation 3:5)

The righteous will be given bodies without sin and that will not be corrupted by sin. Their names will never be removed once they have been written in the book of life.

Promise 6:

> "He who overcomes, I will make him a pillar in the temple of My God, and he will not go out from it anymore; and I will write upon him the name of My God, and the name of the city of My God, the new Jerusalem, which comes down out of heaven from My God, and My new name." (Revelation 3:12)

Jesus promised in John 14:2-3 He was going to prepare a place for us. This place is in the kingdom of heaven, and more specifically, in the city of God, the new Jerusalem. The righteous will be allowed to enter the temple of God and His very presence. The names of God, the new Jerusalem, and the new name of Jesus will be written on the righteous.

Promise 7:

> "Behold, I stand at the door and knock; if anyone hears My voice and opens the door, I will come in to him, and will dine with him, and he with Me." (Revelation 3:20)

Jesus has extended this promise to everyone down through the ages. It is an invitation that requires a response. We must open the door of our heart and invite Him into our life. We can keep the door shut, or we can open it and invite Jesus in. The choice is ours, and He will honor the choice we make. Jesus promised to enter, commune and fellowship with us when we open the door to our heart and invite Him in. He will allow those who open the doors of their hearts to Him to sit with Him on His throne throughout eternity.

JESUS IS OUR HOPE FOR THE FUTURE

God will at a time of His choosing direct His judgments against men and women and the earth, and He will bring this present age to an end. He will destroy the existing heaven and earth and create a new heaven and earth where there will be no sin or suffering. We must acknowledge the reality this can occur at any time in the future. Therefore, we must be prepared by accepting the redemption and reconciliation God extends to us by means of His grace through our faith and trust in and obedience to Jesus

Solomon and other writers present sound and practical advice and wisdom in Proverbs regarding life's challenges and choices. Solomon stated in Proverbs 3:1-12:

> "My son do not forget my teaching,
> But let your heart keep my commandments;
> For length of days and years of life,
> And peace they will add to you.
> Do not let kindness and truth leave you;
> Bind them around your neck,
> Write them on the tablet of your heart.
> So you will find favor and good repute
> In the sight of God and man.
> Trust in the LORD with all your heart,
> And do not lean on your own understanding.
> In all your ways acknowledge Him,
> And He will make your paths straight.
> Do not be wise in your own eyes;
> Fear the LORD and turn away from evil.
> It will be healing to your body
> And refreshment to your bones.
> Honor the LORD from your wealth,
> And from the first of all your produce;
> So your barns will be filled with plenty,
> And your vats will overflow with new wine.
> My son, do not reject the discipline of the LORD,
> Or loathe His reproof,
> For whom the LORD loves He reproves,
> Even as a father, the son in whom he delights."

When we incorporate the wisdom that Solomon and others give to us in Proverbs, we will:

- Find peace in our soul,

- Experience a long life,

- Find favor with God and man,

- Receive health and refreshment for our body,

- Be prosperous, and

- Accept discipline from the LORD with the right attitude.

Solomon encouraged us to turn away from evil, fear God, develop a personal relationship with and be in fellowship with Him, and trust and lean on Him. God will guide and make the paths of our life straight when we do these.

Solomon addressed many important life issues and the futility of things in life that we often incorrectly believe are important in Ecclesiastes. He encouraged us to enjoy life to the fullest and recognize it as God's gift to us. He admonished us to avoid the futility of pursuing things in life that do not have eternal value and direct us away from God. Solomon indicated God has given us life to enjoy while He expects us to live it in obedience to Him. Solomon concluded in Ecclesiastes 12:13-14:

> "The conclusion, when all has been heard, is: fear God and keep His commandments, because this applies to every person. For God will bring every act to judgment, everything which is hidden, whether it is good or evil."

We must enter a redeemed and reconciled relationship with God through faith and trust in and obedience to Jesus to enjoy meaning and purpose in our life. We can find true meaning, purpose and joy only when we enter this relationship and allow the Holy Spirit to transform us into the person God has created us to be. Paul stated in Galatians 2:20:

> "I have been crucified with Christ; and it is no longer I who live, but Christ lives in me; and the life which I now live in the flesh I live by faith in the Son of God, who loved me, and delivered Himself up for me."

We have been redeemed by God's grace through our faith and trust in and obedience to Jesus. God freely extends His gift of redemption to us because of His love, mercy and grace. He promises to place His Spirit in us through Jesus and the Holy Spirit and walk with us as we encounter life's challenges, disappointments and joys. He will prepare our way and enable and equip us to persevere. Jesus is our hope for the future.

EPILOGUE

WHAT JESUS SAID

I asked the Holy Spirit in 1982 to help me better understand God's word in the Bible as it relates to our relationship with Him through Jesus when I agreed to His request to write my initial *REDEEMED BY GOD* book. His assistance over a span of 39 years has given me an understanding of God's word in the Bible necessary to write my series of four *REDEEMED BY GOD* books. I will use words Jesus spoke in the Gospels of Matthew and John to summarize my understanding of the basis for our relationship with God and the redemption He extends to us through our faith and trust in and obedience to Jesus.

I begin with Jesus' statement in John 3:16-17:

> "For God so loved the world, that He gave His only begotten Son, that whoever believes in Him shall not perish, but have eternal life. For God did not send the Son into the world to judge the world, but that the world might be saved through Him."

Jesus indicated God, His Father, made the conscious decision to redeem the world through Him, and this redemption results in eternal life for those who are redeemed. Jesus, as the Son of God, is our Lord who God sent into the world to be our Savior. Jesus stated in John 4:34:

> "My food is to do the will of Him who sent Me and to accomplish His work."

Jesus affirmed His agreement with His Father's decisions to redeem the world through Him even though He knew this decision would ultimately result in His sacrificial death on a cross. Jesus stated in John 8:10:

> "I am the Light of the world; he who follows Me will not walk in the darkness, but will have the Light of life."

Jesus came into the world to show us how to live in a manner pleasing to God and that will result in our receiving eternal life.

Paul indicated in Ephesians 2:8 we are saved by God's grace through faith. He indicated God's grace is offered to us as a gift, and he referred to this gift as being free in Romans 5:15-17. God offers us His grace with no cost to us because we can do nothing independent of His love to obtain it.

Jesus stated in Matthew 5:17-18:

> "Do not think that I came to abolish the Law or the Prophets; I did not come to abolish but to fulfill. For truly I say to you, until heaven and earth pass away, not the smallest letter or stroke shall pass from the Law until all is accomplished."

Jesus confirmed He came to fulfill the Law and the Profits, not to do away with them. Therefore, the Ten Commandments and their extension in the moral law remain to define and convict us of sin.

Jesus stated in John 12:47-50:

> "If anyone hears My sayings and does not keep them, I do not judge him; for I did not come to judge the world, but to save the world. He who rejects Me and does not receive My sayings, has one who judges him; the word I spoke is what will judge him at the last day. For I did not speak on My own initiative, but the Father Himself who sent Me has given Me a commandment as to what to say and what to speak. I know that His commandment is eternal life; therefore the things I speak, I speak just as the Father has told Me."

Jesus reaffirmed He did not come to judge the world, but to save it. He indicated God, His Father, instructed Him to speak the words He spoke, and it is these words that will judge us at the last day. Jesus' words are recorded in the four Gospels of the New Testament. Therefore, we will do well to read, study and internalize them.

Jesus stated in John 10:27-30:

> "My sheep hear My voice, and I know them, and they follow Me; and I give eternal life to them, and they will never perish; and no one will snatch them out of My hand. My Father, who has given them to Me, is greater than all; and no one is able to snatch them out of the Father's hand. I and the Father are One."

Jesus affirmed we know Him and hear his voice when we enter a relationship with Him. He reaffirmed He gives us eternal life, and He stated no one will be able to separate us from our relationship with Him because God, His Father, sustains this relationship.

Jesus stated in John 14:15, 21, 23:

> "If you love Me, you will keep my commandments. ... He who has my commandments and keeps them is the one who loves Me, and he who loves Me will be loved by My Father; and I will love him and will disclose Myself to him. ... If anyone loves Me, he will keep My word, and My Father will love him, and We will come to him and make Our abode with him."

Jesus indicated we demonstrate our love for Him by obeying His commandments and the word He spoke. He stated He will reveal Himself to us, and He and His Father will love and take up residence in us when we do this.

Jesus stated in Matthew 10:37-39:

> "He who loves father or mother more than Me is not worthy of Me, and he who loves son or daughter more than Me is not worthy of Me. And he who does not take his cross and follow after Me is not worthy of Me. He who has found his life will lose it, and he who has lost his life for My sake will find it."

Jesus indicated our love for Him must be greater than our love for anyone or anything that may become an object of our love. Our love for Him must motivate us to obey His words in the Gospels. We risk losing our eternal life when anyone or anything other than Jesus becomes the primary object of our love. We will receive eternal life when we lose our life because of our faith and trust in and obedience to Jesus.

Jesus stated in John 14:1-3, 6-7:

> "Do not let your heart be troubled; believe in God, believe also in Me. In My Father's house are many dwelling places; if it were not so, I would have told you; for I go to prepare a place for you. If I go and prepare a place for you, I will come again and receive you to Myself, that where I am, there you may be also. ... I am the way, and the truth, and the life; no one comes to the Father but through Me. If you had known Me, you would have known My Father also; from now on you know Him and have seen Him."

These are words Jesus spoke to His disciples. He stated He is going to prepare a place for us in God, His Father's, house in heaven, and He will return to receive us to Himself so we can be where He is. Jesus stated we can come to God, His Father, only through Him, and we come to know God as our Father when we know Him.

Jesus stated in John 15:1-6:

"I am the true vine, and My Father is the vinedresser. Every branch in Me that does not bear fruit, He takes away; and every branch that bears fruit, He prunes it so that it may bear more fruit. You are already clean because of the word which I have spoken to you. Abide in Me, and I in you. As the branch cannot bear fruit of itself unless it abides in the vine, so neither can you unless you abide in Me. I am the vine, you are the branches, he who abides in Me and I in him he bears much fruit, for apart from Me you can do nothing. If anyone does not abide in Me, he is thrown away as a branch and dries up; and they gather them, and cast them into the fire and they are burned."

These are words Jesus spoke to His disciples. He stated He is the true vine, and God, His Father, is the vinedresser who will remove branches from the vine that do not bear fruit. Jesus' statement indicated we are to bear fruit in our relationship with Him, and God, His Father, will remove us from this relationship when we do not bear fruit in it. Knowing God will remove us from our relationship with Jesus when we do not bear fruit in this relationship is distressing and a shock. However, God can do as He wills. Jesus indicated we can bear fruit only when we abide in Him, and He abides in us. He emphasized we can do nothing independent of our relationship with Him. Jesus continued in John 15:7:

"If you abide in Me, and My words abide in you, ask whatever you wish, and it will be done for you."

Jesus indicated we can request anything from Him in prayer when we abide in Him, and His words abide in us. He assured us our requests will be granted. They must be compatible with God's nature and character.

Paul stated in Romans 10:8-10 we enter a relationship with Jesus when we profess with our mouth He is Lord and believe in our heart God raised Him from the dead. The Bible teaches we are to grow and mature in this relationship after we enter it. Peter instructed us in 1 Peter 2:1-3 to long for the pure milk of the word so we can grow in respect to salvation. Paul instructed us in Philippians 2:12-13 to work out our salvation with fear and trembling so God can will and work His good pleasure through us. He also instructed us in 1 Corinthians 3:10-15 to build our life on the foundation of Jesus. These actions prepare and equip us to do good works referred to by Paul in Ephesians 2:10 that God prepares for us to perform.

Paul indicated in Romans 12:4-8, 1 Corinthians 12:3-11, 28, and Ephesians 4:11-13 the Holy Spirit gives us supernatural spiritual gifts that uniquely enable and equip us to perform our good works. Our good works are the fruit on Jesus' vine that God prunes so we can bear more fruit.

Jesus instructed us in Matthew 5:16 to let our light shine before men so they can see our good works. Our good works are performed to glorify God, and they are proof of the presence of Jesus and the Holy Spirit in our life.

James indicated we demonstrate our faith by our works in James 2:14-24. He indicated faith that does not result in works is useless; it is dead. Our faith must motivate us to do the good works God has prepared for us to perform as it grows and matures.

Jesus stated in Matthew 7:13-14:

> "Enter through the narrow gate; for the gate is wide and the way is broad that leads to destruction, and there are many who enter through it. For the gate is small and the way is narrow that leads to life, and there are few who find it."

Jesus' parable of the Sower in Matthew 13:1-9 helps us understand His statement. Jesus indicated in this parable that sharing His words with others is like a sower who spreads seeds over the ground. Some seeds fall beside a road and are immediately eaten by birds. Some seeds fall on rocky places where there is little soil. They initially grow, and then they dry up when the sun shines on them because they do not have deep roots. Some seeds fall among thorns, and the thorns grow and chock them when they grow. Some seeds fall on good soil, and they grow and produce fruit. Jesus identified those represented by the Sower's seeds in Mathew 13:18-22:

- **Seeds that fall beside a road** represented individuals who hear Jesus' words and do not understand them. Therefore, Satan deceives and snatches them from Jesus.

- **Seeds that fall on rocky places where there is little soil** represented individuals who eagerly reccive Jesus' words with joy, but they fail to learn what His words mean. They fall away from Jesus when afflictions or persecutions arise. This occurs because Jesus' words do not form the foundation of their lives.

- **Seeds that fall among thorns** represented individuals who receive and understand Jesus' words, but the worries of life and the deceitfulness of wealth overshadow and obscure His words. As a result, they do not produce fruit in their relationship with Jesus. Therefore, God removes them from the relationship.

- **Seeds that fall on good soil represented** individuals who receive, understand, and build their lives on the foundation of Jesus' words. As a result, they produce fruit in their relationship with Jesus. Therefore, they are among the few who Jesus indicated find life.

There are individuals who enter a relationship with Jesus who do not grow and mature in this relationship and perform good works God has prepared for them to perform in this relationship. Therefore, they do not bear fruit in this relationship. This normally occurs because they are not motivated to grow and mature in their relationship with Jesus and perform good works God prepares for them to perform in the relationship. They may also do nothing after receiving God's gift of grace through Jesus because they believe this gift is free, and therefore, they do nothing after receiving it.

There is no acceptable reason for our light not to shine before men as proof of our bearing fruit through our good works in our relationship with Jesus. Therefore, individuals who do not bear fruit in this relationship will be removed from the relationship by God. This will occur when their failure to bear fruit through their good works has not been addressed and corrected before they stand in judgement before God after they die (Hebrews 9:27-28).

I want to return to God's love for us demonstrated by sending His Son, Jesus, into the world so we can receive eternal life after we die. Jesus' sacrificial death on a cross enables God to redeem and reconcile us to Himself by means of His gift of grace.

God gives us the freedom to choose to accept or reject His gift of grace and receive His redemption, and He gives us to the end of our life to make this choice. Ignoring or avoiding this choice has the result of our rejecting God's gift of grace and redemption. The Bible teaches we will be judged by God after we die, and we will be separated from God, Jesus and the Holy Spirit forever when we have not received His gift of grace and redemption. We will initially be in Hades (hell) after we die and then in the lake of fire after the great white throne judgement. The Bible also teaches we enter a redeemed and reconciled relationship with God through Jesus after we receive His gift of grace and His redemption, and we will be with God, Jesus and the Holy Spirit in the kingdom of heaven forever after we die.

Some individuals do not believe or recognize there are requirements when they enter a reconciled relationship with God through Jesus because Paul referred to God's gift of grace as being free. Christian denominations also teach the salvation we receive through Jesus is free. This creates a false perception we do not need to do anything before and after we receive our salvation. However, previous paragraphs indicate, and the Bible teaches there are requirements when we enter a reconciled relationship with God after we have been redeemed by His grace through Jesus.

The Bible teaches God and Jesus bless and reward us when we do what is required of us after we are redeemed by God and have entered a reconciled relationship with Him through our faith and trust in and obedience to Jesus. These blessings and rewards begin while we are alive and continue after we die and enter heaven. The Bible also teaches we will experience God's judgement after we die, and we have done none of these requirements while we were alive.

CLOSING COMMENTS

Moses gave us the Law that established the moral code God expects us to live by. The Law defined sin that separates us from God when it is present in our life. The Law convicts us of sins in our life. It cannot redeem us from these sins and reconcile us to God. Therefore, God extended His love and grace to us by sending us a Savior, Jesus, to redeem us from the consequences of our sins and reconcile us to Himself. Jesus stated in Matthew 5:17-19 that nothing shall be removed from the Law until heaven and earth pass away. This will not occur until the great white throne judgement.

Joshua stated in Joshua 1:8:

> "This book of the law shall not depart from your mouth, but you shall meditate on it day and night, so that you may be careful to do according to all that is written in it; for then you will make your way prosperous, and then you will have success."

It is impossible for us to live a life without sin. Therefore, God sent Jesus into the world to be a sacrifice for and to save us from the consequences of our sins. God forgives and redeems us from our sins through Jesus when we repent of our sins and seek and receive His forgiveness and redemption through our faith in Jesus.

God gives us freedom to choose to or not to seek His forgiveness, redemption and reconciliation through Jesus. We are separated from Him, Jesus and the Holy Spirit forever when we die, and we did not repent of our sins and seek God's forgiveness and receive His redemption and reconciliation through Jesus while we were alive. We will be sent to Hades (hell) after we die and then to the lake of fire after the great white throne judgement. We are redeemed by God and reconciled to Him when we repent of our sins and receive Jesus as our Savior and Lord of our life. We then enter a bilateral relationship with Him, Jesus and the Holy Spirit in the kingdom of God on earth.

God, Jesus, the Holy Spirit and we have obligations in this bilateral relationship. God and Jesus will honor their covenants and promises that are presented in the Bible. We are to spiritually grow and mature as we grow in our faith and trust in and obedience to Jesus. This is a lifelong process. The Holy Spirit facilitates our ability to spiritually grow and mature in our relationship with God through Jesus though our faithful and disciplined study of the Bible. He then equips us to perform good works in Jesus' name that God prepares for us to perform. We secure our entrance into the kingdom of heaven after we die when we perform our good works in service and ministry to others for God's glory because we love Jesus and obey His words (1 Timothy 4:14-16, 2 Peter 1:5-11). God then acts through the Holy Spirit in our relationship with Him through Jesus to make our "way prosperous" and enable us to "have success" during our life.

REFERENCES

1. Grant, R. D. and Wells Miller, A., *Recovering Connections*, Harper San Francisco, 1993.

2. Miller, J. K., *The Secret Life of the Soul*, Broadman & Holman Publishers, 1997.

3. Webb, Chris, *The Fire of the Word - Meeting God on Holy Ground*, IVP Books, 2011.

APPENDIX A
PROPHESIES CONCERNING JESUS

PROPHESIES CONCERNING EVENTS IN
THE LIFE OF JESUS

	Events in Jesus' Life	Old Testament Prophesies	Fulfilled in the New Testament
1.	Born of a woman	Genesis 3:15	Galatians 4:4 Matthew 1:20
2.	Born of a virgin	Isaiah 7:14	Matthew 1:18, 24, 25 Luke 1:26-35
3.	Son of God	Psalm 2:7 1 Chronicles 17:11-14 2 Samuel 7:12-16	Matthew 3:17 Matthew 16:16 John 1:34, 49
4.	Seed of Abraham	Genesis 22:18 Genesis 12:2-3	Matthew 1:1 Galatians 3:16
5.	Son of Isaac	Genesis 21:12	Luke 3:23, 34 Matthew 1:2
6.	Son of Jacob	Numbers 24:17	Luke 3:23, 34 Matthew 1:2 Luke 1:33
7.	Tribe of Judah	Genesis 49:10	Luke 3:23, 33 Matthew 1:2 Hebrews 7:14
8.	Family line of Jesse	Isaiah 11:1, 10	Luke 3:23, 32 Matthew 1:6

9.	House of David	Jeremiah 23:5 2 Samuel 7:12-16	Luke 3:23, 31 Matthew 1:1
10.	Born in Bethlehem	Micah 5:2	Matthew 2:1 Luke 2:4-7
11.	Presented with gifts	Psalm 72:10 Isaiah 60:6	Matthew 2:1, 11
12.	Herod Kills Children	Jeremiah 31:15	Matthew 2:16
13.	Jesus' pre-existence	Micah 5:2 Isaiah 9:6, 7 Isaiah 41:4; 44:6; 48:12 Psalm 102:25	Colossians 1:17 John 1:1-2; 8:58 John 17:5.24 Revelation 1:17, 2:8 Revelation 22:13
14.	He shall be called Lord	Psalm 110:1 Jeremiah 23:6	Luke 2:11 Luke 20:41-44
15.	He shall be Emmanuel	Isaiah 7:14	Matthew 1:23 Luke 7:16
16.	He shall be a prophet	Deuteronomy 18:18	Matthew 21:11 Luke 7:16 John 4:19, 6:14, 7:40
17.	He shall be a priest	Psalm 110:4	Hebrews 3:1, 5:5-6
18.	He shall be a judge	Isaiah 33:22	John 5:30 2 Timothy 4:1
19.	He shall be a king	Psalms 2:6	Matthew 21:5, 27:37 John 18:33-38
20.	He shall be anointed by the Holy Spirit	Isaiah 11:2 Isaiah 42:1, 61:1-2	Matthew 3:16-17 Mark 1:10 Luke 4:15-21, 43 John 1:32
21.	He shall have a zeal for God	Psalm 69:9	John 2:15-17

22.	He shall be preceded by a messenger	Isaiah 40:3 Malachi 3:1	Matthew 3:1-2 John 1:23 Luke 1:17
23.	Jesus' ministry was to begin in Galilee.	Isaiah 9:1	Matthew 4:12-13, 17
24.	Jesus was to have a ministry of miracles	Isaiah 35:5-6	Matthew 9:32-35 Matthew 11:4-6 Mark 7:33-35 John 5:5-9, 9:6-11 John 11:43-47
25.	Jesus was to teach in parables	Psalm 78:2	Matthew 13:34
26.	Jesus was to enter the temple	Malachi 3:1	Matthew 21:12
27.	Jesus was to enter Jerusalem on a donkey	Zechariah 9:9	Luke 19:35-37 Matthew 21:6-11
28.	Jesus was to be a "stone of stumbling" to the Jews	Psalm 118:22 Isaiah 8:14, 28:16	1 Peter 2:7 Romans 9:32-33
29.	Jesus was to be a light to the Gentiles	Isaiah 60:3 Isaiah 49:6	Acts 13:47-48 Acts 28:28
30.	Jesus' resurrection	Psalm 16:10, 30:3 Psalm 41:10 Hosea 6:2	Acts 2:31 Luke 24:46 Mark 16:6 Matthew 28:6
31.	Jesus' ascension	Psalm 68:18	Acts 1:9
32.	Jesus to sit at the right hand of God	Psalm 110:1	Hebrews 1:3 Mark 16:19 Acts 2:34-35
33.	Jesus to be betrayed by a friend	Psalms 41:9, 55:12-14	Matthew 10:4 Matthew 26:49-50 John 13:21

34.	Jesus sold for 30 pieces of silver	Zechariah 11:12	Matthew 26:15, 27:3
35.	Money to be thrown in God's house	Zechariah 11:13	Matthew 27:5
36.	Silver to be used to buy Potter's Field	Zechariah 11:13	Matthew 27:7
37.	Jesus to be forsaken by disciples	Zechariah 13:7	Mark 14:27, 14:50 Matthew 26:31
38.	Jesus to be accused by by false witnesses	Psalm 35:11	Matthew 26:59-61
39.	Jesus to be dumb before accusers	Isaiah 53:7	Matthew 27:12-19
40.	Jesus to be wounded and bruised	Isaiah 53:5 Zechariah 13:6	Matthew 27:26
41.	Jesus to be smitten and spit upon	Isaiah 50:6 Micah 5:1	Matthew 26:27 Luke 22:63
42.	Jesus to be mocked	Psalm 22:7-8	Matthew 27:31
43.	Jesus to fall under His cross	Psalm 109:24-25	John 19:17 Luke 23:26 Matthew 27:31-32
44.	Jesus' hands and feet to be pierced	Psalms 22:16 Zechariah 12:10	Luke 23:33 John 20:25
45.	Jesus to be crucified with thieves	Isaiah 53:12	Matthew 27:38 Mark 15:27-28
46.	Jesus made intercession for His persecutors	Isaiah 53;12	Luke 23:34
47.	Jesus was rejected by His own people	Isaiah 53:3 Psalm 69:8, 118:22	John 1:11, 7:5, 48 Matthew 21:42-43
48.	Jesus was hated without a cause	Psalm 69:4 Isaiah 49:7	John 15:25

49.	Friends stood far off when He was crucified	Psalm 38:11	Luke 23:49 Mark 15:40 Matthew 27:55-56
50.	People shook their heads at Jesus when He was crucified	Psalm 22:7, 109:25	Matthew 27:39
51.	Jesus was stared upon when He was crucified	Psalm 22:17	Luke 23:35
52.	Jesus' garments were parted and lots were cast for them when He was crucified	Psalm 22:18	John 19:23-34
53.	Jesus was to suffer thirst when He was crucified	Psalm 22:15, 69:21	John 19:28
54.	Gall and vinegar were to be offered to Jesus when He was crucified	Psalm 69:21	Matthew 27:34 John 19:28-29
55.	Jesus was to feel forsaken by God when He was crucified	Psalm 21:1	Matthew 27:46
56.	Jesus was to commit Himself to God when He was crucified	Psalm 31:5	Luke 23:46
57.	None of Jesus' bones were to be broken when He was crucified	Psalm 34:20	John 19:23
58.	Jesus' heart was to be broken when He was crucified	Psalm 22:14	John 19:34
59.	Jesus' side was to be pierced	Zechariah 12;10	John 19:34
60.	Darkness was to come over the land when Jesus was crucified	Amos 8:9	Matthew 27:45
61.	Jesus was to be buried in a rich man's tomb	Isaiah 53:9	Matthew 27:57-60

PROPHESIES CONCERNING THE
SECOND COMING OF JESUS [1]

	Bible Verse	Prophesy
1.	Psalm 50:3-6	Jesus will return to execute judgment and to gather His people, Israel, to Himself. Refers to the return of Jesus at the end of the Tribulation.
2.	Isaiah 9:6-7	Jesus will return to rule during His millennial kingdom.
3.	Isaiah 66:18	Jesus will return to gather the nations of the world to Himself. Refers to Jesus setting up His millennial kingdom.
4.	Daniel 7:7-8	Ten-kingdom federation will be formed with the Antichrist as its head.
5.	Daniel 7:13-14	Jesus will be given dominion to set up His kingdom on earth during the middle of the tribulation.
6.	Daniel 7:26-27	The Antichrist will be judged and dominion o of the earth will be given to the followers of Jesus.
7.	Daniel 8:23-25	The Antichrist's power will be derived from Satan. The Antichrist will make war against Jesus, who will defeat him.
8.	Daniel 9:24-27	Tribulation will be seven years. The Antichrist will commit abomination of desolation and break 7-year covenant with Israel during the middle of the tribulation.
9.	Daniel 11:31, 12:11	The Antichrist commits abomination of desolation.
10.	Ezekiel 38-39	Israel will be invaded by the king of the north (Russia) and the king of the south (Egypt).

11.	Zechariah 12:10	Israel will recognize Jesus as her Messiah and will acknowledge with deep contrition that He was the One whom their forefathers had nailed to a cross when He returns to set up His millennial kingdom.
12.	Zechariah 14:1-9	Jesus will return with the armies of heaven to battle the Antichrist and the armies of the kings of the ten-kingdom federation at the battle of Armageddon. He will return by way of the Mount of Olives.
13.	Matthew 24:15-18 Mark 13:5-13 Luke 21:8-9	Prophesies by Jesus concerning the first half of the Tribulation.
14.	Matthew 24:15-18 Mark 13:14-16	Prophesies by Jesus concerning the abomination of desolation during the middle of the Tribulation.
15.	Matthew 24:19-25 Mark 13:17-23 Luke 17:22-37	Prophesies by Jesus concerning the great Tribulation (last three and one-half years of the Tribulation).
16.	Matthew 24:26-41 Mark 13:24-29 Luke 17:22-37	Prophesies by Jesus concerning the rapture.
17.	Acts 1:9-11	Jesus will return in the same way that He ascended to heaven. He ascended from the Mount of Olives to the east of Jerusalem and He will return by way of the Mount of Olives.
18.	1 Corinthians 15:51-52	Jesus will return to gather Christians to Himself at the rapture at the sound of the last trumpet.
19.	1 Thessalonians 1:10	Jesus will rescue us from the wrath of God during the great tribulation.
20.	1 Thessalonians 4:13-17	The dead in Christ will rise first, after which those who are alive will be caught up with Jesus at the rapture.

21. 1 Thessalonians 5:9-10   Jesus will rescue Christians from the wrath of God during the great tribulation by gathering them to Himself at the rapture.

22. 2 Thessalonians 2:1-4   Jesus will return to gather Christians to Himself at the rapture after the abomination of desolation by the Antichrist.

---

[1]   Does not include prophesies in the Revelation of John